How to Steal a Pennant

How to

by MAURY WILLS

Steal a Pennant

with DON FREEMAN

G. P. PUTNAM'S SONS New York

SBN: 399-11699-0

Library of Congress Cataloging in Publication Data

Wills, Maury, 1932–
    How to steal a pennant.

    Autobiographical.
    1. Wills, Maury, 1932–   2. Baseball. I. Freeman,
Don, 1922–   joint author.
GV865.W55A28   796.357'092'4 [B]   75-34442

To Marty Bell, a gifted author and editor, for his invaluable direction in preparing the manuscript for publication, and to Mike Ryan, public relations director of the San Diego Padres, for his expert editorial assistance

CONTENTS

Preface

MAURY WILLS came along ten years too late. They would have loved him in Brooklyn.

Although Maury was close to the hearts of the fans in Los Angeles, he was more the Brooklyn-era type of player.

He had an almost Eddie Stanky quality about him. Maury never made a mistake on the playing field. He was usually, as Charlie Dressen once said, about two innings ahead of everyone else.

Maury had a drive about him that is lacking in most of today's players. In fact, the whole Dodger team of Maury's time had one incentive, and that was to win. The only difference between the Los Angeles Dodgers and the old Gas House Gang from St. Louis was in their language. When Pepper Martin went for a fly ball, he would yell, "I got it." When Gil Hodges went after a pop-up, he would say, "I have it."

They were colorful, exciting teams locked in equally colorful and exciting times in baseball.

The Los Angeles fans came out to see Maury steal a base, Don Drysdale win a game, or Sandy Koufax break another record.

However, the Los Angeles Dodgers, including Maury Wills, were not always all-American boys. They fought among themselves physically and mentally, but maybe that wasn't such a bad thing. Look at the Oakland A's of the 1970s.

When Maury first came up in 1960 from Spokane, our then team captain, Pee Wee Reese, told me, "Buzzie, you've just made your first mistake." Two weeks later Pee Wee admitted he was wrong, and it was not long before the fans knew we had the Dodger shortstop for the future in Maury Wills.

Maury helped the Dodgers not only on the field, but also in the trading market. After only one season in the majors and just 242 at bats, manager Walter Alston and the Dodger brass were convinced that Maury was their next shortstop.

This enabled the Dodgers to trade Don Zimmer, the heir apparent to Pee Wee's position. A deal was made with the club wherein the Dodgers received cash and three players for Zimmer.

The offer was John Goryl, John Hanely, and Ron Perranoski. At first I said, "Ron who? Never heard of him and we don't want him." The Cubs said he was pretty good and they had given him $30,000 to sign.

Reluctantly, we agreed to the deal. When the word got out, the writers wanted to know about the new players. All I could tell then were the names of the first two players and "some left-handed pitcher." I wasn't even sure of the spelling.

Well, Perranoski turned out to be one of the best left-handed relief pitchers in the National League for many seasons.

Given the chance, Maury Wills could become a highly successful major-league manager. Like in 1960, no mistake would be made.

I feel Maury is capable of handling the job and it should be only a short time before he is given the opportunity to prove himself again, this time as a manager.

He has what it takes to become successful. Maury has many interesting theories which I would like to see him try. Some of his ideas seem very sound; there are others, frankly, I'm not so sure about.

I may not, in fact, I don't, agree with some of his notions involving the game and strategy situations as a manager, but I will say this with all sincerity: I respect the baseball mind of Maury Wills.

La Jolla, California   BUZZIE BAVASI
President, San Diego Padres

. . . his legs and feet were speed
and thunder and surprise.
—WHITNEY BALLIETT,

> *in an essay about a*
> *jazz dancer known as*
> *Baby Lawrence*

1

A Fast Pace, a Strong Beat, and Plenty of Excitement

IT was a road game for the Mets, and they were behind by one run in the top of the ninth. The first hitter reached first on a walk. Instead of calling for a sacrifice, Yogi Berra, the manager, had his next hitter swing away, and he bounced into a double play.

The next two batters cracked out singles. And the New York batter after that was out swinging. They lost the ball game.

Later a writer asked the manager why he didn't sacrifice the first runner to second when he had the opportunity.

"For what?" Yogi demanded. "We weren't playing at home."

In other words, he was playing by the book, which says that when you're at home you play to tie, on the road you play to win. That's the book. That's the way it's been done in baseball for the last 105 years. The theory behind this doubtful piece of antiquated strategy is that it's not enough to tie the score because the home team will be coming to bat in the last of the ninth. But it should be obvious to all except book managers that you have to tie the score before you can win, whether your club goes up first or last.

It's a fallacy to assume that the home team hits in

any more innings than the visiting club. What's the difference whether you're playing at home or on the road?

As an NBC baseball broadcaster I've been watching the book managers from the booth and thinking to myself that perhaps I could do better. The very first thing I would do as a major-league manager would be to eliminate the book. The book has got to go. "Play by the book," the tradition tells us. The best answer to that was given by Dick Williams, when he was managing the Oakland A's. "I've never gone by the book," said Dick, "because I've never met the guy who wrote it."

But there aren't many Dick Williams' around. Mostly, the major leagues are full of managers who go strictly by the book.

If you're behind by, say, four runs, the book strategy calls for the long ball. The idea is to get a runner on base and then go for the fences. Drive in some runs; get on the scoreboard. But not on my ball club. Runs come one at a time more often than they do in bunches.

If my team is four runs behind—say it's 4–0 in the first inning—my order would be to forget the long ball. We play for one run and we get it, with bunts and steals and sacrifices. Now it's 4–1. We play for another run in the second inning the same way, and it's 4–2, and we're getting back into the ball game.

Home runs and triples are nice to have, but you don't need them, necessarily, to wipe out a four-run deficit. Waiting for the long ball to happen is what puts gray on a manager's head. But they keep doing it, year after year.

"What, me bunt when we're four runs behind?" they demand, and nobody questions their flimsy logic because it's a part of the book.

Going for the long ball even if your club isn't behind can be just as disastrous. In the first game of the 1974 World Series, the Dodgers were able to put their first two batters on base in the second inning and again in the third. But neither time did manager Walt Alston call for a sacrifice to bunt to move them to second— and none of the first four Dodger base runners in the game was able to score.

It says in the book that when a pitcher has two strikes and no balls on the batter, he wastes the next pitch—but why? It should seem evident that a pitcher wants to keep his throws to a minimum during a game. A Don Sutton, for example, will throw about 120 pitches in a nine-inning game, and he would prefer not to throw any more than that. Most pitchers want to limit their throws. But if he has a 0-2 count going against a hitter and, instead of wasting the next pitch, he slips and the batter cranks out a hit, the book manager goes out of his mind.

So we have the absurd spectacle in major-league baseball of standout pitchers, on that 0-2 count, throwing extra pitches that miss the corners and permit the batter to gain an even break. What happens invariably is that the batter becomes more aggressive and becomes a stronger threat. Most batters are more challenging when they are behind in the count—at least 15 percent more effective in their chances of getting on base. What this means, if my arithmetic is accurate, is by not going for that third strike on a 0-2 count, the pitcher has taken a .285 hitter and turned him into a .300 hitter—and he has done this only to appease the book manager.

The book tells us that you always use a left-handed pitcher against a left-handed batter, which is outdated nonsense. Or from the offensive point of view, you juggle your lineup in a game so that your left-handed hitters won't have to face left-handed pitching. But I'd rather have a .300 hitter who is left-handed going against a lefty than a .250 hitter who happens to bat from the right side. When Ted Williams or Stan Musial went up to face a lefty, no manager in his right mind would have thought of putting in a right-handed pinch hitter.

The book says that you never put the potential winning run on base with a walk. Well, "never" is a long time. Would you have put Dusty Baker, as the possible winning run, on base to get at Hank Aaron? But book managers keep saying in similar situations, "Hell, I couldn't walk that guy. He meant the winning run." The book managers always find a good way to lose.

The book insists that your weak hitters bat in the sixth, seventh, and eighth spots in the lineup. It says that you should rarely, if ever, steal third base. It says that you never put a power hitter into the leadoff position. It says that between starts, your pitchers must always run for their exercise whatever the condition of their legs—you can ruin a lot of heavy-legged pitchers that way. It says that you never steal if your club is behind, and that is utterly wrong. A good base stealer makes it to second, and immediately the move will alter the opposing club's defense. The shortstop must play back in the hole, and that eliminates the force play that might have resulted if the runner had remained on first. And it also eliminates the chance of the second baseman charging to his right for a force play.

The book declares that the only time the first baseman and the third baseman play close to their respective foul lines is in the latter part of a game, in the seventh, eighth, and ninth innings. "Protect those lines," the book manager orders when the possible tying or winning run is on first. But a game can be won or lost in the beginning and middle innings as well as in the final three. With so many one-run victories in big-league baseball today, every run is vital. Why not protect the lines throughout the game?

The book is an institution that serves to protect the manager and puts the player in a position where he gets the blame when things go wrong. The book is a refuge for dull, unimaginative, uncreative, and incompetent managers to hide behind, and it is never questioned. The book is dull and overused. The book is a part of lazy thinking and the enemy of intelligence.

The only way you can steal a pennant is with the smartest team, the smartest playing, the smartest managing. The smart manager plays against the old concept of the book, which is stodgy and predictable, a relic of baseball's past.

As a ballplayer I never played by the book. And I don't live by the book either. I have always believed that the personality of a baseball player is reflected in the way he plays the game. My own personality came out in stealing bases. I was a restless ballplayer. I'm still a restless human being, always on the move. I can't sit still. I like movies and concerts, but I don't have the patience to sit through them.

I like books—I own a large library of sports books, and I flip through each important one as it comes out—but when I sit down to read it, page by page, it isn't long before the old impatience gets to me and I put the book down and I'm up doing something more active.

Speed is a vital part of my life. I'm taking lessons in flying. I like zipping around on my motorcycle. And it gives me pleasure to extend my Jaguar. Once, on the freeway outside Los Angeles, I was caught speeding in my Jaguar. When I was flagged down by the motorcycle cop, he looked at my license, and then he recognized me.

"Maury Wills," he said. Then he shook his head. "What in the hell were you trying to do?"

"I just wanted to see if it would go up to one sixty," I said. "That's what's here on the speedometer as the limit."

"Well, you had it up to one hundred twenty," the cop said. "Isn't that fast enough for you?"

I'm not proud of this, but it's a part of me. I like a fast pace, a strong beat and plenty of excitement.

I like to be with people, and I can't say that I mind being the center of attention in a group, wherever I may be. Frankly, I like being center stage in any surroundings. It is a feeling I always had as a ballplayer, that the eyes of the ball park were on me, that I wasn't merely an athlete but an entertainer. My goal, aside from the obvious one of winning ball games, was to entertain the paying customers. What they wanted to see from me was speed and cunning and aggression and stolen bases. When I'd go for a base, the fans would come alive. Even if I was thrown out, it was still entertainment for them. I always had this sense of wanting to give the fans what they paid for.

By tradition, ballplayers are expected to pretend that they don't hear the cheers of the fans. The book says that you keep your head down no matter how loud the fans are yelling. "Keep your head out of the stands," the old saying goes around the dugout. A hesitant tip of the cap is considered daring, and only a showboat would smile and wave. What a tiresome concept that is! It's boring and it's phony! I always knew the crowd was there, and I knew what they wanted to see, and if I gave it to them and they cheered, I responded the way any entertainer is supposed to do.

Partly, I guess, this inner view of myself as an entertainer has some relation to the fondness I have for celebrities. I like being around my friends in show business, people like Redd Foxx, Mac Davis, Sidney Poitier, Walter Matthau, Ella Fitzgerald, Glen Campbell, Sammy Davis, Frank Sinatra, Buddy Rich, Doris Day. I like their self-assurance and poise, the way they handle life's pressures. I like their spark and ginger. They tend to live life on a higher emotional level, and their excitement is contagious.

I like a certain flamboyance in my life. That's one reason I enjoy living where I do, in the Marina Del Rey section of the Los Angeles area, with the boating set on the Pacific shore. It's less than ten minutes from the LA International Airport, and at least 500 airline stewardesses form a pleasant part of the marina's scenery. Such people as Dan Rowan, the Smothers brothers, Joey Bishop, William (*Cannon*) Conrad, John Wayne, and Frank Sinatra either live here or maintain their boats here. The life-style at the marina is casual and freewheeling, the essence of Southern California. It's an easygoing, free-spending crowd, and the accent is on youth—not all necessarily young people but people whose attitude toward life has a youthful orientation.

I like young people. The truth is that I can learn more from younger people than from the post-forty set. Young people are more flexible and open-minded, and I delight in their company. Still, even though I dress young, I don't pretend to be any younger than I am, which is a foolish and self-deceptive practice. I don't have to pretend—I feel younger now than I ever have in my life.

The record book says I was born on October 2, 1932. (My full name, incidentally, is Maurice Morning Wills. By the time I came along, the seventh of thirteen children, all the good names were gone. I've got a brother named Calvin Coolidge Wills and another, incredibly, named Robert Lee Wills. I was named for an insurance salesman in our old neighborhood, in Washington, D.C. Maurice Morning was his name, and he used to be greeted by my father with, "Good morning, Mr. Morning, how are you this morning? I hope tomorrow morning is as nice a morning as this morning, Mr. Morning." It became a family joke, and I got stuck with it.) My father was a part-time Baptist minister and a full-time machinist. We didn't have too much in terms of worldly goods. I know what hand-me-downs are. Probably that's why I like to live well and dress well and drive the best cars and go to the top restaurants. I like to socialize and I'll accept a Dewar's scotch on the rocks. It all adds up—playing most of my career with a glamor team, the Dodgers, in the most glamorous of ball parks, Dodger Stadium, and living now in glamorous Marina Del Rey.

I'll admit there's a touch of conmanship in me. For as long as I can remember, I've been able to project a little-boy smile and a bit of charm and have it work for me. When it doesn't work, I'm surprised and annoyed, but those times are rare.

Above all else, I am a man of great pride. Other men may take pride in having been associated with something bigger than themselves—the law or medicine or the church or the Marines. I'm proud that I was the captain of the Los Angeles Dodgers, that I was baseball's first $100,000-a-year shortstop, and that, in 1971, I was named the major-league shortstop of the year. I'm proud of my lifetime batting average of .286 and my record of having played in the most consecutive games in one season—165 games in 1962, the year in which the Dodgers went against the Giants in a three-game play-off.

But the accomplishment that gave me the most pride was stealing 104 bases in 1962 for a major-league record. This surpassed Ty Cobb's record of 96 stolen bases, which had stood since 1915 and was generally considered to have been written in concrete.

I'm proud when I read about how I left my mark on baseball, that my base-stealing record changed the face of the game. It opened the way for a new interest in base stealing, a lost art when I came along. Now every club has its share of base stealers. It's also true that as the teams began to move into the new, larger ball parks in the 1960s and '70s, speed and base stealing were added to the offensive tools. And the game became more interesting.

To acquire that record, I endured a lot of pain and anguish. Stealing those 104 bases was a hard-bought record. I liked that record, it was a significant part of my life, and I watched with strained emotions as Lou Brock of the Cardinals made his successful assault, day after day, in the 1974 season.

Throughout that summer, when it became evident that Brock was making a strong run for it, the reporters kept asking me how I felt about it. My phone was ringing every day with calls from writers all over the country.

Well, how *did* I feel? In July, on an NBC telecast of a game in St. Louis, I did an interview with Brock on the field, and I said later on the air, "I wish Lou the best. I hope that if he does break my record, I'll be up here in the announcer's booth describing it."

I meant that—at least I thought I did at the time. A part of me must have rebelled, however, even while I was saying the "right" things. When the writers would ask about the pressure involved in stealing bases, I'd reply, "The pressure becomes worse the more you steal. Those first twenty bases are a lot easier than the last twenty. Lou will really know pressure in late August and September, the closer he gets to my record."

This was interpreted by some people as a prediction on my part that Lou Brock would fold under the pressure. I meant no such thing. I was merely thinking back to the pressure that I had known in '62.

Writers would ask about the differences in our styles. "Brock is fast," my reply went, "but I think I was able to read pitchers better, with more finesse." And that was misinterpreted. One Los Angeles sportscaster told his viewers, "Oh, these modest baseball players. Maury Wills says that Lou Brock may be faster, but he's not as smart."

I was learning firsthand the wisdom in the old saying that a closed mouth gathers no foot Then it came to me that I was probably talking too much in answering the questions. I was overexplaining, overhustling, as we say in the dugout. A reporter would, in effect, ask for the time, and I'd tell him how to make a watch.

Each morning I would check the box score of the Cardinals' game to see if Lou had stolen another one— and usually he had. When he reached the 70s, I began to feel a certain anxiety about my record. I considered 85 stolen bases the striking zone to my record, and once he got past that number, I knew the record would fall because Lou Brock is an excellent base stealer. I was resigned to it then, and I felt no more anxiety as Lou went on to steal his 118 bases.

To a professional athlete, a record is an intensely personal thing. It is a part of one's identity, and I can't deny that Lou Brock, by breaking my record, did chip away at my identity. I'm sure that if Babe Ruth had been alive in 1961, he wouldn't have been overjoyed to see Roger Maris break his home run record of 60 in one year or that the Babe would have been all that thrilled when Hank Aaron hit No. 715 to break his career record.

I think this is a normal human reaction, and it is what I honestly felt. Now, insofar as records are concerned, I'll just have to go on and do something else that is outstanding.

There is something else that I could have been proud of—and that is being a major-league manager. It was what I have always pointed to, and when my playing career ended with the Dodgers, there was nothing I wanted more than the chance to join that exclusive club of managers in the big leagues. But there were no offers. There was, however, an offer from NBC to work as the analyst—a term I prefer over "color" man—on what the network calls the backup TV games, on Saturday afternoons and on Monday nights, beginning in June. (ABC has since acquired the Monday night games.)

The backup game is televised regionally, or, when the main game is rained out, on the full network. For the All-Star game, I became a part of the broadcasting team on NBC Radio.

My broadcasting career had its start in a duck blind near Alamosa, Colorado, in the fall of 1972. I spent a week there with Curt Gowdy and a production crew filming an episode of *American Sportsman* for ABC. We didn't follow a script. All our dialogue was spontaneous.

One very early morning, as we stood in the chill of the duck blind, I said to Curt, "Now that I'm out of baseball, I've always thought I'd like to go into broadcasting. Could the master give me some tips?"

"Well, sure, Maury," Curt said in that crisp, strongly modulated professional voice of his. "The best tip I would say would be to always be yourself. Don't try to pattern yourself after anybody else in the business. All you've got to sell is your own individuality. Nobody wants a copy of anything else. Be natural. Be observant. And sometimes be silent."

It was just idle talk in the morning as we were waiting for the ducks to appear in the gray sky. I was interested in the ducks, but I was more interested in broadcasting.

I kept talking to Curt about the things I could do, the knowledge and background I could bring to the broadcasting profession. I talked about my years as a player and how I could spot things during a game because baseball was so much a part of me. I said I could step right in and do a topnotch professional job.

Curt listened and nodded his head at each of the points as I mentioned them. "There's only one thing that might hold you back, Maury," Curt said.

"What's that?" I said eagerly.

"Lack of confidence," said Curt with a big grin.

We had a great time during that week in Colorado. Curt and I became good friends, and even though we joked about my interest in broadcasting, he knew that underneath my kidding I was serious.

About a week later Sandy Koufax, a great Dodger pitcher who by nature and temperament was never cut out to be a TV sports announcer, notified NBC that he wanted to quit his job as a baseball broadcaster. Then I had several phone calls from Gowdy, from his home in Boston, and he told me that he had talked about my ambitions with Carl Lindemann and Chet Simmons, the top men in sports at NBC. He added that they were indeed interested.

We had several meetings, NBC brought me to New York for a session in the network's high executive echelons, and I was hired. I was a rookie in a different kind of game, and I poured myself into a new profession with the same kind of single-minded dedication that I had given to baseball in my career.

To begin with, I began studying diction, and I tried to slow down my flow of words and give them clarity and definition. I'm embarrassed when I listen to too many ex-athletes on the air, in whatever sport you might name, who assume that their knowledge of the sport compensates for their speech inadequacies, the way they mumble or shout, their inarticulateness on the air, their habit of saying "Y'know" to fill every pause. I also happen to be embarrassed for professional athletes who haven't bothered to improve their speech patterns as they move into the spotlight. They seem to think—if they think about it at all—that being inarticulate is somehow "manly" and that speaking properly is "showboating."

I bought a pocket dictionary, which I always carry with me to study and expand my vocabulary. There's nothing duller than a sportscaster who uses the same words again and again. I only have a high school education, but years of travel and learning as I moved

around have given me what I consider the equivalent
of a college education. You can get an education without using textbooks, but the one book that's indispens-
able is the dictionary. Webster's is my graduate school.
I pounce on new words the way a cat leaps on a ball of
yarn, with zeal and enthusiasm.

I know I've added something to sports broadcasting.
I've heard this from fans, critics, fellow announcers,
people in baseball who like my penetrating interview
questions and my comments on the game. Viewers
especially enjoy my predictions on when a runner will
steal or when a catcher has called for a pitchout. It isn't
done with mirrors. I study the players and their habits
on the field. As an analyst I approach a game as well
prepared in my own way as I would if I were a player
or a manager. I know something about how the game is
played or should be played, and I like to pass what I
know on to the viewers with the highest degree of
professionalism. Whatever I do, I want to be the best.
I'm very aware of what people might say about me. I'm
sensitive to criticism and on the other hand, I glow at
praise. And what I like most of all is to hear a compliment that indicates I've added to both the viewer's en-
joyment of the game and his understanding of its finer
points.

In that regard, broadcasting is highly rewarding,
and I thoroughly enjoy my work. I like the big-league
atmosphere, I like the games and the travel and the
people, and I like the realization that comes with the
inner feeling that I continue to grow both as a person
and in the profession.

Still, I'd like to be a manager of a major-league club.
When there was talk about the possibility of a black
manager in the big leagues, my name kept popping up

around the top of the list, and that pleased me. Obviously, I wanted to be the first black manager. But I didn't make it. Instead, the Cleveland Indians signed Frank Robinson. I was disappointed, but I was happy for Frank, and in fact, I worked for a week at spring training at Frank's invitation in teaching his club my theories on baserunning and base stealing.

The signing of Robinson, by the way, cost me a gourmet dinner. I had bet Mel Durslag, widely syndicated sports columnist of the Los Angeles *Herald-Examiner*, that there would not be a black manager by the start of the 1975 season.

"How much?" said Mel.

"Dinner for four at the best restaurant in LA," I said, confidently.

I lost the bet, and I was happy about it.

Yet—I still don't think the signing of Frank Robinson has eliminated the stigma attached to a black manager in the majors. I see the entire black issue as still being in limbo. Just because the Cleveland Indians saw the wisdom in hiring a black manager, it doesn't mean that baseball's reservations on the subject have been resolved forevermore.

I don't think, for instance, that there will be a parallel between the signing of Frank Robinson as the first black manager and the signing of Jackie Robinson as the first black player in organized baseball in modern times. I don't foresee the rush to hire black managers as there was, to some extent, a flurry of activity in trying for black ballplayers after Jackie proved his value to a club, both on the field and at the turnstiles.

Actually, there wasn't such a big rush to sign blacks in Jackie's wake—it was limited mainly to the National League. This accounts for the general superiority of the National League, too. The top players in the American League are just as good as those in the National, but in the National League there are more of them. After the first two clubs in each division you don't find much in the American League. In the National you will find quality all the way down to the last two clubs in each division.

The National League got the jump on signing the better black players, and the American League never caught up, and they're still paying for it. It's ironic, therefore, that it was an American League club that hired the first black manager. Perhaps they are trying to get even with history.

Just as there was no rule that kept blacks out of organized baseball until Jackie Robinson was hired by Branch Rickey in 1946, no rule ever stated that a big-league club couldn't hire a black manager. But tradition, with its long restrictive arm, had always prevented it.

The number of blacks qualified to manage increases each year. In spite of Frank Robinson, baseball still thinks it's a big gamble to hire a black manager. It certainly isn't a gamble at the most sensitive of pressure points, the gate. Fans have never stayed away from the ball park because blacks were playing, and they wouldn't stay away with a black doing the managing. Fans stay away for one reason—they don't want to be in the same ball park with a losing team, and who can blame them?

There's a subtle difference in why baseball has been even more leery of hiring black managers than of adding black ballplayers. It's a reason that I don't think you will ever hear articulated by any baseball executive, and it is wrapped up in one word—authority. The signing of black players had many elements involved, but authority was not one of them. A manager, by definition, is a figure of authority. He isn't called Skipper because he owns a seagoing vessel. A manager manages; he leads; he barks out orders; he sets rules. Baseball still wonders, it seems to me, whether or not this is a function that's acceptable for blacks, whether or not a black man can be placed in charge of whites. And that is a tradition which is by no means confined to baseball. But if baseball is truly the national game, then it is up to baseball people to be in the forefront of social change instead of waiting for the barriers to crumble elsewhere and then meekly to follow suit.

My ambition to manage a big-league club has little to do with the color of my skin. Being black is no qualification in itself for a manager's job—no more than having white skin pigment should be. But I think it's obvious that where the color of my skin was irrelevant in my playing days, it does matter in regard to my potential as a manager.

How qualified am I? I know I'm certainly as qualified as any of the people whose names have appeared in the paper as managerial material, either black or white. They are all good men—blacks such as Tommie Aaron, who is Hank Aaron's brother, Jim Gilliam, Larry Doby, and the long list of white candidates headed by Tom LaSorda. All are good men, yes, and as I compare our individual qualifications and backgrounds, I have to say I'm as good as any of them. I'd like to have the opportunity to prove it on the field.

If this indicates a pretty strong measure of self-confidence, I won't deny it. If I were handed the reins of a big-league club, I would bring to the job the same maximum of self-confidence that I developed over a twenty-two-year playing career. As a manager I would be confident to issue a prediction right at the start.

Give me a last-place club, and after three years we would be strongly in contention, and by the fourth year we'd go all the way. Give me a club that finished in the middle of the division standings, and—I'll state it flatly—we win it all within three years.

Joe Namath, in his heyday with the Jets, used to guarantee Super Bowls. I'll guarantee pennants.

I will guarantee something else—a ball club under my command would always play exciting baseball and draw customers into the ball park. A ball club has to be an extension of the manager, of his personality and temperament. I was always an exciting ballplayer, and my teams would be a reflection of this in their approach to the game and as an outgrowth of my type of aggressive leadership.

In this book I have outlined the way that I would steal a pennant. My ideas, expressed in print, may not get me a job as manager. But I hope that it serves to wake up a lot of people in the sleeping sport of baseball. I hope they listen and realize how the game can be improved, made more interesting and exciting.

I want to bring baseball fully into the 1970s, and the way to do that is to pinpoint the deficiencies of the traditional attitudes which add up to the book.

I say, throw out the book. This is the new book.

2

Aggressive Baseball—Fighting to Win (A Tale of Tigers, Hell Raisers, and Pranksters)

A BASEBALL team has to have an overall philosophy. A team is not twenty-five players playing their own game, but twenty-five guys working. You begin with an overall philosophy, and the key word in that philosophy is aggressiveness. By aggressiveness, I am referring to much more than stealing bases. Aggressiveness applies to every aspect of team play. I want players who put on their uniforms aggressively.

A manager can teach the mechanics of the game. He can teach judgment, but it's more difficult to teach aggressiveness. Contrarily, it's easier to tone down an overaggressive player than it is to instill that quality into a safety-first athlete. As a player and broadcaster I've seen too many safety-first ballplayers lacking the decisiveness that makes winners. On the base paths they are always stealing glances at the coaches instead of stealing bases; they play it safe, and they lose. I wouldn't want any losers on my ball club.

As I see the role of a manager, the job involves six major areas: (1) setting up an offense and arranging a lineup; (2) putting together a defense and a pitching staff; (3) handling players on and off the field; (4) acquiring personnel through trades; (5) handling the press; and (6) hiring coaches.

31

It is an accepted tradition in the baseball book that for his coaches a manager hires old cronies, old card-playing, beer-drinking buddies. To hell with that. My coaches would be chosen for their knowledge and teaching skills. Moreover, they would have authority. My players would understand from the start that the coaches are the manager's fingers, that their orders are to be followed.

A coach must have some juice going for him. In major-league baseball today, players wouldn't hesitate to tell a coach to go to hell. And I say that's the manager's fault for not establishing the coach's authority from the beginning. But the ultimate authority, of course, lies with the manager. In common with Gene Mauch and Billy Martin, I would list myself among the managers who insist on running the show. I wouldn't want coaches who are second-guessers.

Four coaches would do the job for me—one at first base, one at third, a pitching coach, and a fourth coach who would, in a sense, be my alter ego, my second set of eyes, and I'd want him sitting next to me on the bench. His function is to know the manager's style and philosophy in every detail, to issue a reminder when, for example, the manager is too occupied with other matters to notice that an outfielder is playing too deep—or a reminder that the opposing club has its powerhouse hitters due to bat in the next inning, and so on. They are reminders, in short, that expand a manager's vision and his capacity for leading and the team's capability of winning.

Such a man would be invaluable. There aren't too many of them around, but I can think of one and his name may be unfamiliar to even the most rabid of baseball followers. He is Sam Hairston, a veteran of twenty-five years in baseball who never got out of the minor leagues. I played against Sam in 1954, when I was with Pueblo, Colorado, in the Western League. He's now a scout in the White Sox farm system. Sam is a man of intense loyalty and dedication, he can teach, he knows the game from the inside, and I'd want him sitting next to me on the bench. Sam could help any team. I'd want him to help mine.

Sam Hairston also happens to be a black, and that brings up another issue. I'd want at least one black on my coaching staff. Just because he's black? Exactly. It seems to me only right that given a position of authority, I give an opportunity to a black who fits my standards of what a coach should be. Too many qualified black players for too long have been denied the opportunity in coaching that is their due on the basis of ability and service to the game.

Certainly there are black coaches in baseball today, and it infuriates me to see where they are most often put to work—time after time you see them at first base. There you see them—Ernie Banks, Elston Howard, Jim Gilliam, Larry Doby, men of enormous capability placed in a position of the least authority, where the fewest decisions must be made. It's nothing more than baseball's version of tokenism, and it's deplorable.

If there is a place for a buddy on a coaching staff, it is at first base. It's a good spot for an ex-player who has been around the game but has never achieved much in the way of stardom. Still, he would have to know the meaning of aggressiveness. I don't want any safety-first coaches either.

At third base I'd like to have Benny "Cananea" Reyes, another unfamiliar name. Reyes is a Mexican who has played and managed and won in the Mexican winter league. He coached for me at Hermosillo, and I'd match him against anyone in the major leagues for baseball knowledge and insights. The third base coach must be able to think quickly, he has to be able to anticipate what the manager wants, and he has to execute. His decisions must be exactly the same as those a manager would make under the same conditions. He has to be so in tune with a manager's thoughts that they are inseparable. The two minds must travel along the same wave length. I can't conceive of anyone better than Benny Reyes.

For a pitching coach, there would be few more qualified than one of the smartest catchers I've ever seen— John Roseboro, my old Dodger teammate, whose specialty was handling pitchers. With a topflight corps of veteran pitchers, there is less need for the teaching type of coach. Given a young staff, however, I'd like a Red Adams or a Ron Perranoski or a Jim Bunning, all of them men of vast patience, who can counsel and steady young pitchers, correct their mistakes, and instill confidence.

On some major-league clubs one coach will perform as a liaison or a mediator between the manager and the players. What this means to me is that the manager himself has slipped in his vital function of communicating with the team. Walt Alston used to say, "You don't win games in the clubhouse. You win on the field." True, the game is played on the field, but winning, creating, and sustaining an aggressive spirit do begin in the clubhouse, and it's in the clubhouse where a manager communicates. No manager who is communicating properly with his players is ever in need of a liaison. Or, to put it differently, if a player feels the need of a liaison, a mediator among the coaches, you can bet that it's the manager who has failed. A team that requires a liaison won't even come close to stealing a pennant.

Spring training, for a manager, is where it all begins. Spring training, on all too many clubs, is where the manager says to the rookies, "Take it easy, fellas. Just get into shape these first few days. We can tell just by looking at you what you can do." And the rookies, naïve in the ways of the game, believe him. They take it easy, and the next you hear of them they are taking the bus out to Shawnee and another season in the minors.

Such tactics go by the book, and they run counter to my philosophy of managing. I would tell my rookies to pour it on from the start. I'd tell each rookie, personally and in the clearest language, to go out there on the first day and work as though his career depended on it because as sure as an accordion player wears a shiny ring when he plays "Lady of Spain," it does.

At spring training, before the sun sets on the first day, I would lay a copy of the baseball rulebook on every player on the squad, veteran and rookie alike, with orders to start studying because I'm going to ask questions later.

How can you play a game without knowing the rules? I have a long-standing suspicion that if they were ever given a test of the rules of the game, 95 percent of all major-league players would get a flunking grade. Most of them—I'd give odds on it—wouldn't even score a gentleman's C.

Only once to my knowledge has a rulebook test ever been given to a major-league squad. This was back about fifteen years ago at camp in Vero Beach, Florida. We all took the test, which consisted of a quiz on rules and game situations—all of us, from manager Walt Alston on down, including the coaches.

We were told later that only one grade of 100 percent was recorded. I have to take a bow for that perfect score, and I will. We were never told how well the manager and coaches did, but I have my suspicions.

Professional baseball players simply don't know the rules. They know the distance between bases is 90 feet, and they know it's 60 feet and 6 inches from the pitcher's mound to home plate. But after that they have to start thinking.

Ballplayers don't even know how big a base is. This is more than a trivia quiz item if baseball is your business. How can a player steal a base and guage his slide if he isn't sure of the dimensions of his target? And if you don't steal bases, you aren't going to steal any pennants. A base is 15 inches across.

Twice a week, at least, we'd have tests on the rules. By opening day my ballplayers would know the rules the way an umpire should (but doesn't always). The most obscure rule can win you a ball game. Or lose one. I'll cite just a few.

I'd want my team to know, for instance, that if you're on first base and running and you tag second and you're on the way to third and the outfielder makes a fantastic catch and you have to retreat back to first, you must retag second base. If you fail to touch second base going back, you are out—but not automatically, only if the opposing team notifies the umpire and if he sees the play. Umpires don't always see plays.

If an outfielder catches a fly ball and he has complete control, then he takes a step and hits the wall and drops the ball, the batter is safe—how many ballplayers know that? Before the batter can be called out, the outfielder must come up with the ball out of his glove. If he collides with another outfielder, the same rule applies.

After all the talk about the infield fly rule, ballplayers could explain it to you as easily as they might converse in Afghanistani. They don't know, either, that a player can run into a dugout to catch a ball. So often a player will stretch out, standing on the step, and he reaches into the dugout and the ball tips the edge of his glove and dribbles away. He shakes his head and runs back to his position, and the fans say, "Good try. Man's out there hustling."

What I say is: "Give that lunkhead a rulebook and tell him to study!" So long as the player retains his footing, he can enter the dugout to catch a foul fly. But once he loses his footing, even with the ball in his glove, and he slips and falls, the ball is dead, the batter is out, and everybody advances a base.

I could go on at length about the rules that most players don't even know exist. As the saying goes, what you don't know can hurt you.

As a ballplayer with hopes of one day being a manager, even before I reached the big leagues, I kept an observant eye on the managers I played for, watching their style and their methods. From Lefty O'Doul, I learned about the casual style, which wasn't for me. Lefty O'Doul was a great hitter in his time, with a lifetime average of .349, and he led the National League twice in hitting. Managing the old San Francisco Seals for seventeen years, Lefty was known for the way he developed young players. One of his protégés was Joe DiMaggio, who went from the Seals to the Yankees.

But by the time I was playing for him, at Seattle, in the late fifties, Lefty had apparently lost his enthusiasm. He would wander into the clubhouse about an hour before game time and look around. Then he'd point to the players, one by one.

"You're pitching today, you're catching, you bat first, and you bat second," and so on until he had his starting lineup. Then he'd tell one of his coaches, "Take care of things. I'll be back later."

About the third inning Lefty might be back in the dugout asking, "What's the score? Are we winning?"

One night we were playing the Hollywood Stars in old Gilmore Field in Hollywood. I had hit safely, and I was on first base. The next batter hit one hard to right field, and it looked like a double at least. I rounded second and tore down the baseline for third, expecting the coach either to stop me at the base or to wave me into home.

Lefty O'Doul was coaching third that night. But where was he when I needed him? There was Lefty, casually leaning against the box seats behind base, talking to Forrest Tucker, the actor. He glanced up, waved me on home, and then resumed his conversation. That was old casual Lefty.

From Bobby Bragan, at Spokane, I learned intensity and the value of a manager who has more than a touch of the teacher. Without Bobby Bragan, I doubt that I would have ever advanced to the major leagues. My hopes were getting pretty thin by this time, after seven years in the minors, and the general feeling was that I had leveled out as a ballplayer.

During batting practice one night Bobby watched me at the plate. The truth is that I was in the middle of a seven-year slump. For the fun and variety of it, I swung from the left side of the plate and hit a few pitches on the nose but with little power.

Bragan stepped into the batting cage. He was no casual manager. Bobby was always breathing fire. "You ever hit left-handed before?" Bobby asked.

"Hell," I said, "it's all I can do to hit the ball right-handed."

"Try it," Bragan suggested. But it was more like an order.

Then he moved into the batter's box. "From here you're three steps closer to first base," he said.

I knew that. Everybody in baseball knows that. I just didn't know that such information would ever benefit me personally.

For the next few days Bragan would pitch to me in batting practice while I hit left-handed. We'd get to the ball park an hour early, and Bobby threw and threw, and I kept swinging away. We were at it steadily for four days, with Bobby shouting instructions.

On the fifth day we were in Sacramento for a series with the Solons. "You're a switch-hitter," Bragan told me in the dugout before the game. "So switch-hit."

For the first time, in that game, I batted left-handed against a right-handed pitcher, and I went away with two hits. I learned that your vision is more direct and you do have perhaps a split second more when the ball can be seen. When you bat from the left side against a right-handed pitcher, when he throws a breaking pitch you see the ball from the moment he begins his delivery.

Four years later, on Memorial Day, playing for the Dodgers against the Mets, I hit a line-drive inside-the-park homer, batting left-handed off Bob Moorhead in the fifth inning. In the ninth, batting right-handed against a lefty, Wilmer "Vinegar Bend" Mizell, I caught a high fastball and sent it sailing into the upper deck. I was practically delirious as I ran around the bases.

It was a memorable Memorial Day since I became the fourth player in the National League and the sixth in the majors to hit a home run right-handed and another homer left-handed in a single game. And it was the result of Bobby Bragan's patience, teaching ability, and capacity for knowing observation, all qualities that a manager should cultivate.

I learned something else from Bobby Bragan—a manager's personal equipment had better include a sense of humor. One night in Phoenix we were complaining loudly in the dugout about the oppressive Arizona heat. Finally, Bragan's temper snapped.

"I'm sick of all this bitching about how hot it is," Bragan shouted. "The next guy who bitches about the heat, it costs him fifty dollars. Let's play ball."

Then Bragan sat down and pulled out a handkerchief and wiped a sea of perspiration from his brow. It was a monstrously hot night.

For two innings there wasn't a whisper about the heat. Then Art Fowler, one of our pitchers, got up from the bench and said, "My God, it's hot!"

Bragan looked up, scowling. But before Bobby could utter a word, Fowler came back with: "And it's just the way I like it!"

Bragan laughed. We all laughed. And I think we won that game.

Aggressiveness takes many forms and has many outlets. I point to the Oakland A's, winners of three straight World Series, as the shining example of a ballclub whose aggressiveness explodes into fighting among themselves. The Dodgers of my time were very similar. From the middle of the 1959 season through the mid-sixties and back again in the early seventies, we were the Oakland A's of our day, the wild bunch of baseball. But nobody knew it.

This was a team of tigers, hell raisers, and pranksters. We were a team of braggarts—we were good and we knew it—and we had our jealousies and feuds and fights. And yet, beginning in '59 and into the sixties, we won four pennants and a world championship. The record will also show that when we didn't fight among ourselves, we didn't win. I'm inclined to think there is a definite connection.

You would have to say we were a fun-loving club. Once, at spring training, general manager Buzzie Bavasi had ordered a costly shipment of assorted seafood delicacies and arranged a big social luncheon in honor of Mrs. Walter O'Malley, the wife of the owner. Don Drysdale, a pitcher with a sense of humor, got wind of the luncheon, and he pulled one of the best steals of his career—he sneaked into the kitchen and hauled the seafood to a nearby beach on the Florida shore, sharing his loot with the Dodger ballplayers. Buzzie was furious.

It was Buzzie who was also involved in one of the zaniest cases of mistaken Dodger identity. This happened one winter when Bavasi read in the sports pages that one of his star outfielders, Tommy Davis, had just scored 30 points in a basketball game. He hit the ceiling.

"Get me Davis on the phone," he said to his secretary.

Soon Buzzie was saying, "Hello, Tommy? Listen, you stupid SOB, what the hell's wrong with you—

fooling around playing basketball? You could get hurt and blow your career. Or don't you care? Look, if all you're interested in in life is a job for fifty dollars a week, I'll fix that up for you."

"Yeah, sure, I'll take it."

"Fresh SOB," Buzzie snapped.

"No, I'll take the job—fifty dollars a week's not bad."

Buzzie hung up, fuming.

· Later he learned that since he hadn't specified which Davis he wanted, his secretary assumed that he wanted Willie Davis, another Dodger outfielder—and Willie Davis happens to have a brother named Tommy Davis, who just happened to answer the phone.

I look back on those years, and I'm astonished that so little of the brawling nature of the Los Angeles Dodgers, our true personality, found its way into print or on the air. A good relationship with the press is obviously helpful to a manager. Everybody seemed to be on our side in some kind of unspoken handshake of silence, which couldn't have been better. Even the Chicago police were with us.

Once, while we were in Chicago to play the Cubs, Walt Alston was roused out of bed at four in the morning by a phone call from the downtown precinct. One of our pitchers, Johnny Podres, was in jail. Johnny, a left-hander and a free spirit, had been disturbing the peace of a Near North Side bar. He was celebrating the sunset or some other event that called for a series of toasts. He ended up in the slammer.

Walt hailed a cab and went down to the station, where he must have said the right words to the police. Podres, red-eyed and full of apologies, was released in the manager's custody. Alston chewed him out and put him to bed.

The next night—they play only day baseball in Chicago, and the nights stretch out like an open invitation—Podres was out celebrating the sunset again, disturbing the peace of the Windy City. Again Alston was awakened by the police.

"He's here again, Mr. Alston," the desk sergeant said. "We've got Podres here. What do we do with him?"

"Let him sleep it off," Alston snapped and rolled over in his bed.

To the best of my recollection, not a word of this appeared in the papers. Maybe the Chicago police were Dodger fans.

This was the Dodger era of Don Drysdale and Sandy Koufax, Duke Snider and John Roseboro and Charlie Neal, of Roger Craig and Jim Gilliam, and the rest. Walt Alston had himself a handful. Unlike losing clubs, where the players shrug off defeat in an air of resignation, we were always a contending team, fighting for every edge.

It was the only team where arguments could be ignited while the manager met with the pitchers to study the opposing lineup.

Walt would name their leadoff hitter.

"Pitch him low and away," one pitcher would say.

"No, goddammit, he murders 'em low and away," another pitcher would say. "High and fast and inside is how you pitch to him."

And then the argument would start, with the other pitchers joining in with noisy opinions. Finally, Alston decided that the best way was to give the batting card to the starting pitcher and ask, "How the hell you going to pitch 'em? You tell us, and we'll try to defense 'em."

Whatever they threw, our pitchers knew that we

wouldn't be able to supply them with many runs. We were sorely lacking in heavy lumber. In one road series, Don Drysdale remained at home in Los Angeles because of an injury. Sandy Koufax had just pitched his second no-hit game. The score was 1–0.

Drysdale phoned Koufax to congratulate him.

"Way to go, Sandy," Don told him. "By the way, did we win?"

We *had* won the game, but considering the way we hit, it was a reasonable question.

Still, we were an arrogant lot, and soon I became as arrogant as any of my teammates. They called me Mouse, but I was really a tiger. One day at Dodger Stadium I was on first base and ready to go for second, with Jim Gilliam at bat. The pitcher threw to first about ten times, and I could see that Gilliam, standing at the plate, was getting impatient.

I took a shorter lead, hoping the pitcher would throw to Gilliam and give him a chance to hit. He whipped two strikes past him. On the third pitch, I stole second. Gilliam, taking the pitch, was called out on strikes. In disgust, he threw his bat down and stormed over to the dugout, glowering at me. It was his way of saying that I had shown him up.

When the inning ended, I was still at second. Gilliam ran out to the infield, and I stepped in front of him.

"You do that again, and I'll stomp you right through the ground," I said.

"Up yours," Gilliam said.

"When this inning's over, I'll see you in the runway," I said.

"A pleasure," Gilliam said.

When we were in the runway that leads to the dugout inside the stadium, Gilliam pointed his finger in my face. In my neighborhood that was the gesture of challenge.

I grabbed Gilliam by the collar, and I had him suspended in the air against the wall. Just as I went back with my fist, the world's biggest outfielder separated us. He was Frank Howard, who stands 6 feet 6 and weighs 240.

Frank grabbed both of us by our collars. "What are you guys doing?" he demanded. "You guys can't fight. We're all on the same team."

He held us in the air for a few seconds, and then he dropped us.

Tommy Davis and I once went under the stands at County Park in Milwaukee. Earlier we had left the hotel and we were on the bus going to the ball park. I was wearing a new V-neck blue pullover sweater and I thought I looked resplendent, but the color scheme offended Tommy Davis' sense of style, which was strictly Early Good Will.

"Where'd you get the sweater, Mouse—at some fire sale?" Davis said in his loud voice.

Ballplayers have a way of talking loudly in the bus when they're looking for the entire ball club to share in their performance. For all the would-be Henny Youngmans on the club, the team bus is the big room.

I said, "What the hell's it to you?"

"The Mouse got a sweater at a fire sale!" Davis persisted, laughing at his own brand of wit.

When we left the bus at the ball park, I pulled Davis aside. "I'll see you under the stands," I said.

Tommy Davis is a bit over 6 feet and weighs at least 200 pounds. He looked down at me. "Any time," he said.

But he kept going into the clubhouse. He sat down in front of his locker and started to undress. I went over to him.

"You and me, Tommy D. Now."

He rose to his feet, and the two of us went out the door, down the stairway and out to a secluded area beneath the grandstand.

I put up my fists like a vest-pocket Muhammad Ali. "Either you're going to whip my ass or I'm going to whip yours."

"Forget it," he said.

"You got something to tell me now about the way I dress."

"Listen, what have I got to win?" Davis said. "You beat me, I couldn't live with that, and it's not going to happen, no way. If I beat you, everybody'll say I'm bigger. I can't win. Why fight?"

"You want to apologize?" I said, my fists still clenched.

"I said, forget it, Mouse."

He turned his back on me. We walked back to the clubhouse in tight-lipped silence. By the time we arrived at our lockers the other Dodgers were already in uniform. They hadn't even missed us.

We went out and played the game, and we won it, going away. Tommy Davis had a hell of a day for himself, with two hits and four runs batted in. I got my two bats and stole three bases. Neither Tommy nor I ever mentioned the incident to anyone, and not a word entered the press.

But there was always a coolness between us. In another game I had received a sign from the bench to tell Davis in left field to move closer to center. I passed the sign along. Davis didn't budge, looking straight at

me. I kept signaling to him. Then he made a finger gesture that said, among other things, "Get off my back,
Wills."

Now the inning had ended, and we were in the dugout. I approached Davis. "Listen," I began, "you saw
me give you that sign out there. Why didn't you—"

In mid-sentence, he was on top of me, and I was hitting back. Before any good punches could be thrown,
though, our teammates had separated us, and the incident, in full view of the fans, was over. There may
have been two sentences about it in the papers.

One of our Dodger squabbles did hit the press. This
goes back to my first full season with the club, in 1960.
We were going through our pregame workout in the
Los Angeles Coliseum. I was at shortstop.

The way fungoes are hit to the outfield, the balls to
the right are tapped when the second baseman has left
his position and has moved near the bag and to the left
when the shortstop has moved close to second base.
The reason is obvious—if the ball isn't hit high
enough to the outfield, there's no danger of an infielder
being struck and possibly injured.

On that day Norm Larker, who was moving in on Gil
Hodges as the Dodger first baseman, was out of the
lineup. So Norm was hitting fungoes—and he was hitting straight out to left, but hitting them when I was in
my position. One of his line drives whistled by, close
to my head. Two more tore past me.

"Dammit, Lark, be careful," I hollered.

Larker was frustrated and angry about being out of
the day's lineup. He yelled back at me, "If I hit you,
Wills, you won't come and get me. You got no guts,
Wills."

Then he flipped the ball into the air, swinging away,

and cracked a stinging liner that whipped past my head and nicked the peak of my cap.

I threw down my glove and ran to the dugout, where I found a ball. I ran to within ten feet of Larker, and after taking dead aim, I threw at his ribs. I missed. The ball hit him full force in his left knee, and he went down in pain, swearing.

Larker is bigger than I am—who isn't?—and thinking as fast as I ran, I figured I had one way of evening the odds. My secret weapon was to get into the clubhouse, where the concrete floor is slippery, and I'd put on my crepe-sole shoes. Then I'd have traction in a fistfight. All's fair in love and baseball fights.

In the clubhouse my lockermate, John Roseboro, looked up. I spilled out the story in a few words.

"Larker'll be here any minute," I said. "I'll be ready for him."

Roseboro shrugged. "You're on your own, my friend," John said.

I threw off my spikes and laced up my crepe-sole shoes. Then I heard the sound of spiked shoes clacking down the runway. It had to be Larker. He strode into the clubhouse looking like Wyatt Earp coming through the swinging doors of a frontier saloon, tough and mean, his fists knotted. But I had my crepe-sole shoes.

"You little son of a bitch," Larker screamed. "Look at my goddamn knee!"

"I told you to be careful," I said. "You damn near hit me."

Some of the players moved in, and one of them reached out and pushed Larker. What he was trying to do was agitate and get the fight going. Larker was thrown off-balance, and he fell into me.

I started punching, and I hit him a good one across the cheek. Larker couldn't get any traction going, with his spikes. He was slipping and sliding, but he could still hit, and he came back with a right cross on my eye.

It must have been a ridiculous sight. There I was in full uniform, with crepe-sole shoes on my feet. And there was Norm Larker flailing away, trying to maintain his footing on a concrete floor. And the other players were in a circle, hollering encouragement.

At this point, Frank Howard moved in as the peacemaker, and he tried to grab me from the back. I whirled around, one of my elbows caught him on the jaw, and down he went. *Ring* magazine would have judged it an accidental TKO.

We stopped swinging at each other, Larker and me, and we stared down at Howard, who had a puzzled look on his face.

"You . . . you guys," Frank said. Then he threw his hands in the air.

We started laughing and apologizing all around, and the incident was forgotten—until the story ran in the papers the next day. But it would have been a bigger story with the A's or the Yankees or the Mets or the Cubs. We were the protected Dodgers.

Years later, in the spring of 1974, I was working with the Dodger rookies as an instructor in baserunning and base stealing. We were at the Dodgertown camp in Vero Beach, Florida, in the midst of the palmettos, the scrub pines, and the palms. It was a bright, sunny morning, and I was walking off the field, with springy steps, humming.

Spring training may be the best of all times for a professional baseball player or even an ex-ballplayer who's now an instructor in the skill he knows best.

Time seems to stand still, and the world is young again.

As I walked into the press room, ahead of me stood Walt Alston and one of the Los Angeles writers, Bob Hunter of the Los Angeles *Herald-Examiner.*

I stopped and greeted the skipper and the writer, and then I started to move on.

"Maury," said Alston. He lifted his head in a beckoning gesture.

I turned around. "Skip?" I said.

"We've been talking about difficult players," Alston said.

He paused, looking straight at me, and then Walt said in flat, even tones, "You know, Maury, you weren't the easiest little prick to manage."

I looked for some indication of the friendly needle, some sign of lighthearted ribbing. But there was none.

I had no answer for Walt Alston. I stared into his cool, humorless eyes. My stomach seemed to sink within me. I walked away quickly, my mood suddenly turned leaden.

You weren't the easiest little prick to manage. No, I suppose I wasn't. I knew I was arrogant and hardheaded. But then was Jim Gilliam easy to manage? Were Tommy Davis, Willie Davis, Roseboro, Snider, Drysdale, Koufax, Neal, Zimmer, and quite a few others on our club? Were *any* of us easy to manage?

In spite of his remark—and I'll admit it cut deeply—I learned an invaluable lesson from Walt Alston in how to be a manager. With that team, under those circumstances, his policy in regard to our brawling and hell raising was the right one: Alston knew when to look the other way.

Before one of my NBC broadcasts in 1974 I was talking with a sportswriter who told me about his team, "What a great bunch of gentlemen they are. If you go in the clubhouse after a game, you wouldn't know whether they won or lost."

He was talking about a last-place team. There were no fights on that team because nobody cared. We cared, on the old Dodgers. The tone of *our* clubhouse was usually like a pot boiling, with various arrogant and hardheaded personalities in conflict. Yet our anger would almost always be funneled out against the opposition on the field. We fought in the clubhouse, and we won on the field.

If you're going to fight yourselves, you had better have a manager who knows how to handle the outbursts—and you had better also have a team with talent. The A's have proved it, in the early seventies. We proved it, we quarrelsome Dodgers, in those pennant-winning sixties, and they were the best years of my life.

3

Offense, Firecrackers, and a Fighter Named Cobb

I'D like to be able to say that the most important player on the field is the shortstop. It's not modesty that forbids—just the facts. Actually, it is the pitcher who controls most ball games, and therefore, the idea of an offense is to wrest the control away from him, to make him and his team feel that the offense has the upper hand.

In order to accomplish this, an offense must have a style, a personality. Style is something that a team develops not in one game, but in a season or over many seasons. And then the team's style precedes them into town. The Yankees with Mickey Mantle and Roger Maris, for instance, had a style based on home run power. The Pirates of recent years had a style related to a lineup with .300 hitters from the leadoff down to the pitcher.

Both teams, of course, won pennants with their styles, but both are lacking in dependability and consistency. As much as I would want to have a home run hitter or two on my club, even if a player clouts 60 home runs in a season, that's only one every three days—it's possible that he's striking out or popping up when he isn't hitting homers. And how often in a manager's career can he assemble a team that has eight starting .300 hitters?

The only constant in baseball is speed. And for me, this is the element to build a style around. Intimidate the pitcher with speed and surprise. Make him feel that he must keep every batter off base, because as soon as one gets on, he's going to be moving around those bases.

People often think that the home run is the *most* intimidating offensive weapon, but I disagree. To me, the best tool to use to unnerve the pitcher is the bunt, the most neglected tool in baseball.

A good bunter in baseball is getting to be as rare as a maker of buggy whips. In the upper echelon of the major-league bunters, I would give strong marks to Ted Sizemore, Bud Harrelson, and Don Kessinger. Only Harrelson plays at least half his games—the home schedule—on natural grass, which is an asset to a bunter. It's much more difficult to control a bunt on artificial turf. On the other hand, for a chop hitter—a close relative to the bunter—the new artificial surface can be an asset in slashing out well-placed pokes through the infield.

I would operate my major-league camp as I would an instructional camp for kids. And I would teach everyone on the team to bunt.

Take a look in any batting cage before a ball game, and you will see the players—pitchers, especially—practicing their home run swing, trying to batter down the fences with their power. In a game, the pitchers won't even touch the ball, but they're all Hank Aarons in the batting cage. Never in my entire career have I ever seen a major-league pitcher practice how to bunt. Not once.

I've seen them bunt because in practice it's customary to bunt twice. But they merely waltz through the motions. Then, having satisfied tradition, they grab the bat by the handle, get a toehold, and aim for the fences.

Maybe it's the old *machismo* notion—they think it's more "manly" to hit a home run, just as they would rather strike a batter out with a blinding fastball than a change-up. There's no glamor in placing a bunt, except to your manager, who has a victory to his credit because a bunt worked and led to the winning run.

I'd have my pitchers bunt, and I'd have my No. 4 slugger bunt too. Try to name one cleanup hitter in either league who is also a good, reliable bunter. Hank Aaron, possibly. Not many others that I can think of.

With men on base, the power hitter should be able to bunt to sacrifice runners to second or third. With runners on first and second with none out and the cleanup hitter at bat, the crowd yells for a hit. How they'd love to see this player hit the long ball.

But if he overswings, he can also hit into a double play. The cleanup hitter is usually not a fast runner, for one thing, and the odds are that he'll hit the ball hard. If the ball is hit hard to the infield, the odds are he will be doubled up, and the rally is over as quickly as a station break.

Instead, if the slugger bunted and sacrificed the runners to second and third, chances are the pitcher would intentionally walk the fifth batter to load the bases for a possible force-out at any base.

Now the sixth and seventh men are coming up, and they're expert bunters. They're playing for me, and they had damned well better be expert bunters. We pull a squeeze play; the run scores. We score by going against the book.

In this situation the book manager will tell his slugger to hit away. By going by the book, he has protected himself, and even if a double play is the result, it is difficult to argue with him.

It should be easy for a power hitter to learn to be an expert bunter. Sluggers are natural hitters. They could use the same good timing, rhythm, and coordination to bunt well. What's more, the odds favor the slugger in a bunt since the infielders are usually positioned deep for them.

But just try telling that to a slugger, and you get a glower that indicates you've sharply questioned his manhood.

I would expect the batters at the top and bottom of the order to be better than merely good bunters—they would have to be expert. And the same applies to the pitchers. A pitcher is supposed to be the real thinker on the team, the high IQ man. A pitcher should be smart enough to know that a well-placed bunt can win him a ball game. And he has to know how to place it.

There's no big mystery to bunting. You just stand comfortably at the plate, keep the bat parallel to the ground, and realize that anybody can do it—with hours and hours of concentrated practice. But isn't it worth it?

Bunting can be most effective when the opposing team has moved players out of their normal positions. There were times, for instance, when the Giants would move catcher Ed Bailey over to first base to keep him hitting in the lineup. We bunted him out of his mind. When the Reds want to give Johnny Bench a rest from catching, they put him at third base. Bench is a superb athlete, but he's no third baseman. I'd have my team bunt him silly. Or else I'd have them fake a bunt, lure him in close, and then slap the ball by him. This can also be done with a pitcher. Draw him in with a bunt stance; then poke the next pitch through the middle.

The bunt can be a weapon for keeping the opposition off-balance. When your club has piled up a solid lead of, say, five runs, the book says you don't pour it on. "Take it easy, guys, let's just get this game over with," they say around the dugout. I call that honeymoon baseball, and to hell with that. We're five runs ahead; they expect us to hit away; we bunt instead.

Baseball is primarily pitching and hitting. If you can pitch or hit, they'll find a spot for you on the club even if your hands turn to antlers when the ball is hit to you. Dick Stuart lasted for years in the major leagues on his bat alone. The way he played first base, people were afraid he'd be an instant casualty out there.

When the Yankees came up with Elston Howard to catch, they had to find a place for Yogi Berra. Now Yogi was a tremendous catcher in his day, but when his reflexes slowed down, they put him at third base or left field because they wanted his bat in the lineup.

Managers will talk about how valuable a player is to the club because of his fielding, but the payoff still comes at the plate. It's one of the unwritten laws of major-league baseball that a good fielder who can't hit is just holding down the job until somebody comes along who can hit consistently. The weak hitter is in there on a temporary pass. If it's "good field, no hit," as the old scouting report has it, it's back to the bush leagues.

They say that the border line batting average today for an infielder (except, of course, the first baseman) is .250. The time-honored cliché goes: "If he's a great fielder and he hits .250, he'll be up there in the big leagues for a long time." You can mark that down as a

very large lie. The truth falls more along these lines—
if you're a great fielder and you're hitting .250, let
someone come along who can hit .280 and can't field
quite as well, and you'd better pack your bags.

Once a man is on base, the next step is to move him
around. Stealing bases lies at the heart of my style of
offense. Stealing intimidates the opposition, excites
the team and the spectators, and brings people into the
ball park. It charges up a ball game. And it wins pennants. Lou Brock, in 1974, almost carried the St. Louis
Cardinals to a division title on his base stealing alone.

I would want every player on my team to know how
to and look to steal. And I would spend a lot of time
teaching them the art.

Lesson No. 1. Forget the old geometric rule that a
straight line is the shortest distance between two
points. In running bases there are no straight lines.
The quickest path around the bases requires cutting
the corners, being able to hit the bag on the inside tip
every time.

Lesson No 2. Forget about speed. One of the least
understood aspects to base stealing is speed. To be a
good base stealer, you don't have to have blinding
speed. You don't need the speed of a Lou Brock, a Willie Davis, or a Herb Washington. Even average speed
is good enough. What's most important is knowing
how to get a good lead and good jump on the pitcher.

Speed is simply overrated. Put a group of players in
a straightaway 100-yard dash, and the winner might
not be the fastest man going around the bases. I've
seen few players better at going from home to first than
Julian Javier of the Cardinals, but in a straight race
Willie Davis could probably beat him.

In my playing days I was never considered the fastest man in the league, but I never lost a footrace. I'd go up against the lean, tall, and graceful-looking players who had the appearance of track stars, and I'd get the jump on them, and once I was out in front they would only push me into running faster.

Several times over the years I challenged Lou Brock to a race. "Let's go, Lou," I'd say as we talked before a game. "Let's have it out. One race to end it all. You and me."

"You don't mean that, Maury," Lou would say. "You really want to race me?"

"Anytime," I'd say.

Then he'd laugh and I'd laugh, and somehow the years passed and we never did race. I wish we had.

Once, in Miami, in 1953, I was timed running from home around the bases in 13.4 seconds. People said that was the world's record, but there was only one time clock in use at the time. That made it unofficial because two clocks are required to put a record into the books.

A good base stealer must be decisive and know all the pitchers and their moves. These are characteristics that can be learned. I studied the pitchers closely and knew their mannerisms thoroughly, so I could "read" them easily. I never hesitated. I started out at full speed.

Writers erred in thinking that I had what they called a light slide. It may have looked as if I were skimming across the infield dirt. But it didn't feel like a light slide to me. My right leg was always bruised. In 1965 I was 30 games ahead of my record-setting base-stealing pace of three years earlier, but my leg started bleeding internally. I had to stop stealing bases in August. I've always thought that if I had not been stopped by a recurrence of the hemorrhaging, I could have stolen 140 or even 150 bases that year.

The worst fault I've observed in watching players try to steal is the way they slow down before a slide—that's fatal. In running, I would have but one thought on my mind: Think of the next base. My target was the outside corner of the next bag. I never slid into a base touching more than that outside corner. When they went to tag me, all that was open to touch was the tip of my toe.

In pictures this would resemble the old hook slide, but the pictures were deceptive because they were taken after I had completed my slide. And it wasn't the fadeaway that Ty Cobb used. I would always hurl my body low to the ground and to the outfield side of second base. When I went into my slide, the foot that I intended to use for tagging the base would be extended straight ahead. Then, as I went into the bag, the momentum would carry me forward, the knee bending away—and the toe reaching for the tip of the bag.

Once you make up your mind to go, go. There's no way a runner can start changing his mind in the middle of the base path. It's impossible to pause and still steal a base: And fear of failure has to be eliminated. I think the instinctive thing is to be cautious, to play safety-first baseball. But the good base stealer must force himself to be aggressive.

Whenever I was picked off by the pitcher, I knew that I had to come back the next time around with even more daring and aggressiveness. It was important that the next time I got on base, I try to steal immediately. It became a challenge, and it was also necessary for me to condition the pitchers to respect me.

There are basic things to look for in *all* pitchers, and

there were individual things I'd seek out in *each* pitcher. My practice was always to watch the pitcher for at least fifteen minutes as he took his warm-up tosses. I'd learn from observation which pitches he made from the stretch position and so on.

Every smart ballplayer has to be observant. During a game I'd always watch the pitcher as he moved around on the mound. A pitcher will usually have good moves or bad moves; there are remarkably few in between. There were some tough ones, such as Warren Spahn and Juan Marichal and Larry Jackson whom I faced, and a number of comparatively easy ones—by "easy" I mean pitchers who gave me confidence that I could get a good lead and a good jump without being picked off.

Odds vary with different runners and different pitchers, but I always felt that if I started to steal second base, I had an 85 percent chance of making it even on the tough pitchers. Those are pretty good odds. But any time that I was struck by the slightest inkling of self-doubt, the odds went down to 60 percent for making it against 40 percent for getting caught. And those aren't good odds at all.

When I first came into the league, the accepted theory was that left-handed pitchers were the most difficult to steal on. This was based on the fact that a left-hander faces the runner at first base as he takes his set position. It was also believed that a left-hander's move was deceptive when he would step toward home plate but throw instead to first base.

By careful observation, I learned that if you have to wait to see where he's going to step, it's too late to steal a base anyway. A left-hander's right foot faces the plate. When that foot goes down, no matter where he throws, the base stealer has to be long gone.

A right-hander has his back to the runner, which means his visibility toward first is lessened. But the runner can't see his moves, and a pitcher can perform some tricky maneuvers with his hands when you're unable to see them.

The toughest pitcher of all for me to run against was Warren Spahn, a left-hander. But he would have been just as tough going right-handed. Spahn's moves were so deceptive that I often found myself guessing—and that's when I learned that guessing with any pitcher, left-handed or right, isn't good enough. It is all psychological, but when you feel you are guessing, the odds go against you.

Although Spahn was the toughest pitcher for me, I never made this information public during my career. I didn't want to give him, or any pitcher, a psychological edge.

My first inkling that the book was wrong about left-handers' being the most difficult for a base stealer came one day in the early '60s. I saw Curt Simmons, a left-handed pitcher with the Cardinals, looking right at me at first base. I said to myself: "How long has this been going on?"

I could steal on Curt Simmons in a breeze, especially when he was throwing to Smokey Burgess, who put his signs out in front so far they could easily be seen from first base. I could pick my pitches for stealing, and I would choose an off-speed pitch—a curve, a change-up, maybe a slider. A fastball reaches the catcher with more velocity and is usually not a stealing pitch.

With Smokey Burgess behind the plate, I could read the signs as though they were being shown on the scoreboard. But with another catcher, I would figure out what the odds were that the pitcher would throw an off-speed pitch, and this was dictated by the count on the batter.

The best count for a stealer is when the pitcher is behind the batter. If the pitcher is ahead with two strikes and no balls, he is in the right spot to throw a pitchout and the runner can get himself nailed.

A good stealing count is two balls and one strike or three balls and one strike. However, if the pitcher has two strikes and no balls on the hitter, he might decide to waste the next pitch and the base stealer could go because a wasted pitch often means a slider or curveball in the dirt. That means the catcher must go down and trap the ball, which is a boon for the base stealer. On the other hand, some pitchers like to use a fastball high and tight as the waste throw.

Pitchers are highly predictable creatures, and they follow the book, chapter and verse. It's their predictability that makes them so vulnerable to the players who become good base stealers by taking the time and effort to study the pitchers' moves and act on them.

Hitters do study the pitchers, and the same knowledge should be used on the base paths. Ted Williams said long ago that it was necessary for a batter to "read" a pitcher's mind and force him to throw the pitch that's easiest to hit. It's just as necessary for a base stealer to "read" pitchers to learn their patterns of throwing. They might throw the first pitch inside, the second one goes for a corner, then it's a breaking ball followed by a fastball, and then another breaking pitch, and so forth, all in a highly predictable series.

Pitchers call this "mixing 'em up." To a runner it can be an open book.

Surprise is always the key element. It's one dictum

in the book that if a game is seemingly in your back pocket, tradition holds that you're not supposed to steal bases. But I say you should steal any time the opposition doesn't expect it, whatever the game situation. Sometimes you steal simply for the sake of aggression. Sometimes you steal to keep the other team off-balance. Sometimes you steal for the sheer exhilaration of it.

Home runs create excitement, but base stealing stirs a very special kind of exhilaration in both the runner and the fans. A home run is a sky rocket. Stolen bases are firecrackers. I just can't forget the wonderful feelings I got from stealing bases.

It was a warm autumn afternoon, and we were playing the San Francisco Giants in Dodger Stadium in the final game of our play-off series for the 1960 pennant. Juan Marichal was pitching for the Giants, and he was always tough for me to steal on because he would always be throwing to the base as hard and low as he could. Juan could throw a ball no higher than three inches off the ground. Willie McCovey, at first base, would catch the ball and slap it at me with his big glove. I can still feel the bruises.

By the eighth inning we were ahead, 3–2. There were two outs. I had stolen one base so far. Then I stole another one, making it to second. Normally, with two outs, I wouldn't attempt to steal third, but the statistics show that there are at least nine different ways that you can score from third that you can't from second.

My thinking went like this: *If I get to third, I can score on a passed ball or a wild pitch or an infield error. Hell, I might even steal home.* So I took off for third. Ed Bailey, behind the plate, threw late, and the ball slipped past third baseman Jim Davenport and went bouncing into left field. I made it home easily.

I had stolen my third base of the day and the 104th of my career. As I ran to the dugout, the fans and my teammates were standing and cheering and I had a big smile on my face. But the smiles disappeared an inning later after our pitching collapsed and we blew the game and the pennant.

About a week before that day, we played our 156th game and I needed two steals to break Ty Cobb's record. There was some dispute at the time about my record because by then the leagues had expanded and we were playing a 162-game season. Ty Cobb stole his 96 bases during a 154-game season, but that year, 1915, the Tigers were involved in two ties and they had to play two extra games. Actually, then, Cobb set his record in the 156th game.

The night before that game Commissioner Ford Frick ruled that I had to break the mark in 154 games to make it official. But later Frick made this statement: "It's a record. Whether we say it's a record in a hundred and sixty-two games or not, there's no question it's a record—the most bases ever stolen in a season."

All season long, I'd been thinking about the record in terms of the same 156 games that Cobb had played.

I remember that night clearly. The weatherman had predicted rain, and to help him out, the groundkeepers had put a lot of water in the dirt around first base. It had become a custom around the league to turn that area around the bases into a swamp to keep me from stealing.

That morning I read in the sports pages that Curt Simmons would be pitching for St. Louis, and I was overjoyed. I could steal off Curt Simmons running backwards. Curt didn't like to throw to first base—or any base, for that matter. When he did throw to a base, he would always step back first and then make his move. As a result, he was an easy mark.

As I sat in the clubhouse, waiting for the Cards to finish batting practice, one of the players came in from the field.

"Dammit," he said, "Simmons is out. He hurt his arm. They're going with Jackson."

Larry Jackson! Batting against Larry Jackson, I must have hit about .105. With his slider, Jackson was a very tough pitcher for me. When a right-hander throws a slider to a left-handed batter, the pitch comes in like a fastball and then slides in at the wrists. They say that the slider was developed by a pitcher who was trying to throw a curve and threw it with too much velocity. But his curve didn't break very much, so at first they said it was just a "nickel curve." But a slider is worth a lot of money to a pitcher. The ball literally slides at the last second, and it snaps across and downward.

Larry Jackson had one hell of a slider. He also had a questionable balk move that was rough on a base runner. He got away with it, though, because he was a veteran. A young rookie coming into the league with that move would have been jumped on by the umpires. But with Jackson throwing, the umpires would just say, "That's his natural move."

I said to Tom Gorman, the umpire, "What the hell's the difference whether it's natural or unnatural? It's still a balk."

"Play ball," Gorman explained.

There was a tremendous amount of excitement in the air that night. Sportsman's Park, an old ball park, was packed, and this was one of the few times when I noticed so many black people in the stands. They were there to see me break Ty Cobb's record.

The first ball that Jackson threw to me was called a strike. I think the entire ball park booed the umpire. It was very unusual—the home team gets a strike on the opposing team's leadoff hitter and the ball park was booing the umpire. But the fans wanted me to get on base and steal.

On one of Jackson's sliders that was coming in at my fists, I managed to get my bat out in front, and I tapped the ball down at the ground. It hit the dirt hard and bounced over Jackson's head out into center field.

I had made it to first, and now Jackson went into his questionable balk maneuver, but the umpires ignored it. Jackson kept wheeling around and throwing to Bill White at first base.

Bill White is now etching a television career in New York, a nice man to have for a friend but then he was a typical major-league first baseman. By that I mean he was a big guy who was always coming down hard on a runner with his mitt. Even if you're standing on the bag, a major-league first baseman will pound you on the arms or legs or ribs.

On one of Jackson's pickoff throws White came down so hard that I had to duck headfirst or else it would have been like a guillotine.

I got up and said to White, "What are you doing to me, brother?"

"Only off the field," White said, "*that's* when we're brothers."

When Jackson began concentrating on the next hitter, Jim Gilliam, I took my maximum lead and broke for second. Carl Sawatski's throw to Dal Maxvill was wide, and I slid in to tie Ty Cobb's record. I was stranded at second when Gilliam, Duke Snider, and Tommy Davis went out in order.

By the seventh inning we were behind, 11–2. Walt Alston said to me, "Forget about the score, Maury. If you get on, steal."

With two outs, I went up against Jackson and his miserable slider. The ball park came to life again. The first pitch was a called strike on the outside corner. The fans booed. I foul-tipped the next pitch, a slider at the fists. Jackson threw two pitches that just missed the corners. I fouled off several more. Then another wide one made the count three and two.

Now I was looking for the meanest slider Jackson could throw. I was set for it. I even pulled away from the plate, and I swung. The ball wasn't hit too hard, and it rolled between Bill White at first and Julian Javier at second. White dove for the ball and just barely missed, and I was on first with a base hit.

Suddenly, all the Dodgers were perched on the front step of the dugout, and across the field the Cardinals were up, too. Jackson paid no attention to Jim Gilliam at bat. He must have thrown to Bill White a dozen times. I decided this was an occasion for a delayed steal.

In a delayed steal you take a much shorter lead to give the appearance that you have no intention of going for the base. My lead was no more than five feet. Jackson figured that I wasn't going, the catcher and infielders relaxed momentarily, and he went into his stretch and fired to the plate.

While the ball was in flight, I took two short steps and ran like a thief. By the time they realized I was stealing I was halfway down the base path. Thirty feet from second base I left the ground and dove headfirst. I was about ten feet short, and I crawled the rest of the way. The throw bounced five feet in front of second base and rolled past it.

I remember lying on the ground with that bag in my hand for about thirty seconds. "This is mine," I kept saying to myself, "and I earned it."

They halted the game. A ground crew came out and took the bag out of its mooring and replaced it with another bag. In the ninth inning the game was halted again when I went up to bat and the public address announcer presented me with the bag and a big sign that said "97." It was a nice ceremony, and we posed for the photographers. As he gave me the bag, the announcer said, "And, Maury, you won't have to steal this one."

I can still hear the deafening roar of the crowd. I felt as light as air.

The record went into the books with an asterisk, but I feel it belongs to me with no arguments.

Base stealing is an offensive tactic that tends to demoralize the opposition even more than the home run. Aside from the pitcher, the defense can do little to prevent the home run. But the base stealer gnaws so annoyingly at a team that every possible measure is adopted to stop him. In my time, at San Francisco they used to turn Candlestick Park into a swamp from excessive watering of the infield, especially around first base. And that's how manager Al Dark, when he was with the Giants, got the nickname of Swamp Fox. I can't say I enjoyed playing much in the swamplands of Candlestick.

The Braves had their own system when Joe Torre

was playing first base. Torre would flop down in front
of the bag while the ball was on its way from the pitcher on a pickoff. I would dive headfirst for the bag, I'd
be blocked, and he'd tag me out.

The first time I was picked off by Torre I hollered at
the umpire, who happened to be Stan Landes, not one
of my favorites.

"He can't do that!" I yelled.

"Why, of course he can," Landes said.

Back and forth we argued, and the fans in Milwaukee were booing me as though I had taken away
their beer-drinking privilege. I realized quickly that
this was one argument I had no chance of winning.

The next day, borrowing a leaf from Ty Cobb, I
bought a file in a hardware store and I filed my spikes
to an edge. When I made it to first on a single, I waited
for the pitcher to try his pickoff move. I took a substan-
tial lead, and when the pitcher threw to first, instead of
diving for the bag, I slid high.

Meanwhile, Joe Torre had gone down on one knee to
block the base. Then he saw me coming, spikes high.
He jumped up and out of the way, and my spikes
ripped into the bag. When I pulled my spikes out, the
stuffing popped right out of the bag.

Torre didn't say a word. He nodded at me as though
the message were plain. We had an umpire who didn't
know how to enforce a rule, and that meant I had to
protect my rights on the base paths. The rule is specific
on this point, that no baseman can block a base until
he has possession of the ball. The only player who can
get away with blocking the base is the catcher—with
anyone else it's interference. Or it should be if the umpire knows enough to enforce the rule.

The next time I was at first base the pitcher made at

least five pickoff attempts. On the last one, Joe was blocking the base again, and I tore into him on the knee.

Torre hobbled over to the Milwaukee dugout, which is on the first base side. Except for our first base coach, I was alone out there, and I looked over at the Dodgers' dugout for help in case war broke out. About five minutes later Torre returned with his leg and uniform taped, but there was still blood all over his knee. Joe Torre is a big hairy bull of a man, and I was afraid he would pinch my ear off.

But Joe didn't even nod. He went back to his position. I assumed he knew that whenever a baseman blocks the base path, he's vulnerable, and he accepted that. For this reason I always had great respect for Joe Torre as a professional.

Joe was also a catcher, and he was, incidentally, the only catcher in the league who ever spoke to me when I came to bat. It's the custom in baseball for the catcher to greet the hitter the first time he comes to bat. But catchers resent base stealers, and except for Joe Torre, none of them ever gave me a nod.

But Joe was not one to forget. When he was catching and I was running into home, he would make me eat dirt. Torre wouldn't just tag me with the ball; he tried to pound me into the ground with it. All part of the game of stopping the stealer.

For most kids, when they first get into baseball, their heroes are the big sluggers, a Hank Aaron or a Mickey Mantle or a Willie Mays. It wasn't until I was well into my career in professional baseball that I became aware of the player who would influence me most. He was Ty Cobb, one of the greatest ballplayers ever to put on a uniform—some say the greatest of them all. He was the fightingest, most aggressive, most explosively exciting player in history, and it is one of the regrets of my life that I never met him.

Once, in 1959, when I was playing for the Spokane Indians against the Phoenix Giants in a Coast League game, Ty Cobb was a spectator in the stands, in a seat above home plate behind the screen. But I didn't see him. It is a strange feeling to have, this realization that Ty Cobb's eyes were on me as I stole two bases against Phoenix that night. I didn't even know he was there until the next day, when I read an interview with Cobb in the Phoenix paper.

In the article Cobb said about me, "I like the way that kid slides." That was high praise from the master.

Ty Cobb was an incredible athlete and an extraordinary man, and by reading his autobiography and studying everything I could lay my hands on about him, I enriched my knowledge of baseball. Over a twenty-four-year career, playing in 1,500 games, Cobb had a lifetime batting average of .367. He led the American League in hitting for twelve seasons. All told, he put no less than twenty records into the books.

Cobb was a ferocious competitor, the snarlingest, toughest ballplayer who ever lived. He would sharpen his spikes with a file until they were lethal weapons. There's one Ty Cobb story that typifies the man. Once a pitcher threw at him, barely missing his chin. On the next pitch Cobb carefully topped the ball to the first baseman, who flipped it to the pitcher on the run toward first.

As the pitcher tagged the base and saw Cobb coming at him, he kept on running for the stands. Cobb went after him. Just as the pitcher tried to leap the barrier,

Cobb left his feet and slid high at the pitcher, and his spikes ripped him across the flanks.

It isn't recorded whether that pitcher ever threw again at Cobb, but I'm inclined to doubt it.

Cobb was a wildcat on the bases, always applying the pressure, but he was also a thinking man's ballplayer. One of the Cobb theories that I put to use as a player was that it's always easier to make great plays against great players. The reason is a matter of predictability—the great player is expected to make the right moves, while the mediocre player won't respond in any way that it is possible to predict.

But it's the great players, of course, who take away your strength. For instance, if you're at bat and Brooks Robinson is at third base, he is so skillful at fielding bunts that you have to be leery of going at him.

Along similar lines, it's mainly the good base runners who get picked off. Only the good base runner is daring enough to take a long lead and risk being tagged.

Ty Cobb was thoroughly unpredictable. He drove pitchers and catchers crazy because they knew he would steal, but they didn't know how he would do it. Once Cobb had been thrown out by a young catcher on an attempted steal. The next time at bat, Cobb said to the catcher, "I'm going to steal every base on you, better be ready." Then he poked a single through the infield. Settled at first, Cobb taunted the catcher and then stole second on the first pitch. He yelled out again from second base and promptly stole third. After a loud warning he stole home—touring the bases on four pitched balls.

He drove infielders crazy because he had such incredible control as a hitter. He was the best bunter in baseball. But if the infielders came in close, he'd slap the ball through an opening. Cobb used a choke grip on the bat, with his hands spaced several inches apart, and he knew how to punch the ball wherever he aimed it. He drove the outfielders berserk because they knew he could stretch a single to a double or a triple, and they would make foolish throws.

He could have been the game's greatest home run hitter if he had so chosen. In one game, just to prove he could do it, he went for the fences and hit three home runs.

As a big man—Ty was about 6 feet 2 and weighed 190 pounds—he could intimidate players, and with his size he could afford contact. With my 159-pound frame when I first hit the big leagues, I couldn't afford Cobb's rough tactics in stealing bases. If I had been as big as Cobb, though, I would have made him look like a nice guy. They called me the gentleman stealer, but I was just as angry and defiant and arrogant as Cobb ever was.

I had great admiration for Ty Cobb as a stubborn fighter. When Cobb first came up to the Tigers as a rookie, he brought his favorite bats, which he had soaked all winter in linseed oil. One morning he discovered that one of his teammates, Sam Chapman, who resented the arrogant rookie, had broken all his bats. Cobb was furious.

He charged into the clubhouse and went after the first veteran he saw, a man who outweighed him by fifty pounds. For once he was overmatched and Cobb was beaten to a bloody pulp as the other players stood around and watched. But the player who administered the whipping to Cobb came to admire him so much for not surrendering that he became his friend and his champion and won the rest of the team over to Cobb's side.

When Cobb was on the road, fans of the home city club would gather beneath his hotel window and keep him awake nights with their noise. Whenever the Tigers left the hotel to enter the team bus, there were always anti-Cobb fans who had to be pushed aside by the police. In the ball park, when he was in the outfield, people threw rocks at him.

Cobb carried his anger to the very end. He never retired from baseball. He just never played another game because he was suspended. Cobb was a fighter, and he fought for things that players accept today as their right. In Cobb's day it was a rule that players paid their own medical bills during the season. Cobb fought against that and finally forced the Detroit Tigers' management to pay for his medical expenses. In time this practice became commonplace.

Even in his last year, playing for Connie Mack and the Philadelphia A's, Cobb was contemptuous of authority. During a game one day, as Cobb was about to go to the plate, he was stopped by Mack's gentle voice.

"Ty," said Mack, "you've been in a slump. I was just wondering—"

"You were wondering—what?" Cobb snapped.

"Well," said Mack, swallowing nervously, not wanting to say the words, "I was just wondering how you'd feel if I sent in a pinch hitter."

"Nobody pinch-hits for Cobb!" Ty hollered. Then he picked up a bat, stormed to the plate, and savagely lashed into the first pitch for a clean, crisp single to left.

That was Tyrus Raymond Cobb. When I broke his base-stealing record, one of the newspapers ran a big pen-and-ink drawing of me sliding into a base, with Ty Cobb looking down and smiling in approval. I liked that image very much. I liked the Cobb style of offensive baseball, and it will be a part of any team that I ever manage. Ty Cobb knew exactly how to steal a pennant.

4

Pitching Is the Heart of Defense

AS the Oakland A's proved in the 1974 World Series, the key to championship baseball is defense. And defense begins on the pitcher's mound. When I was with the Dodgers, Sandy Koufax would call us over before a game he was to pitch and say, "Just get me one run, and don't get fancy out there."

A Sandy Koufax is as rare as the Kohinoor diamond and, to a manager, just as valuable. A complete introvert and an extremely private man, Sandy was difficult to know. But I think I came as close as anyone to penetrating the shell that Sandy had unwittingly put himself into over the years. After he had pitched a game, Sandy and I would often be the only Dodgers in the training room tending to our various ills, Sandy with his arthritic arm, me with my battered legs. We would be alone for hours, talking, exchanging views on life and baseball. Gradually, his guard came down, and he revealed much about himself; in the process, I learned not only about Sandy, but about the psychology of pitching.

Pitchers see themselves as finely tuned Swiss watches, and to some degree they are. They deserve some pampering as the heart of a ball club. But nobody could pamper a pitcher more than he pampers himself. The average pitcher thinks about his arm as much as an opera singer thinks about his voice.

An outfielder can play with a double Exedrin headache and still hit home runs. But most pitchers have to be 100 percent physically and emotionally, or they won't start. Koufax heads the list of exceptions—he always played hurt—and that list would include Don Drysdale and Bob Gibson and Juan Marichal, all of whom ignored their minor ailments.

Pitchers experience a wide range of emotions, from supreme confidence to total anguish, as they stand on the mound. Claude Osteen, a Dodger left-hander, once told me, "You go out on that mound, and you don't know what in hell's going to happen. You can feel terrific warming up and get pounded out of the box in the first inning. Sandy Koufax could beat a ball club single-handed, but the rest of us need eight other guys to help us. You're all alone out there. It all depends on you. You're the one who gets the win or the loss in your record. And you just work every four days—that gives you too much time to think. That means a helluva lot of worrying."

Claude said that pitchers were different from other ballplayers because they had to face what he called the "fear of the unknown."

I experienced these feelings as a pitcher at Cardozo High School in Washington, D.C., where I won twenty-five games and lost two. I went to major-league tryout camps to try to make it as a pitcher.

At one camp I struck everybody out and the New York Giants told me they'd sign me if I were 20 pounds heavier and 4 inches taller—I was 5 feet 10, about 160 pounds. They were interested only in size, not strikeouts. In the early years of signing blacks, teams were looking only for perfect black players. One weakness, such as size, and you were out of consideration.

So I became an infielder. In my rookie year with Hornell, New York, in the Pony League, I fell into a slump. I couldn't buy a hit with a certified check. I asked Doc Axelson, our manager, if I could pitch. He sent me up against the Hamilton, Ontario, club. I thought I had a hopping fastball and a deceptive curve, but I was hit hard from the first pitch. In the first inning we fell behind, 5–0. The bases were full; no one was out. Doc came out to the mound.

"I'll have to take the ball, Maury," he said quietly. He was a kind man.

I was a typical young pitcher. "I got this next guy's number," I said, holding the ball tightly in my hand. "I'll get out of it, Doc."

Doc paused. "All right, one more chance."

With the bases loaded, I could move into my full windup. I went with my best pitch, my blinding fastball. Instantly, I heard the smack of wood against leather—the line drive damn near flattened our third baseman and kept rising into left field, heading for the North Pole.

I didn't wait for Doc. I started walking to the dugout, my head hanging. I threw down my glove, and then I went into the clubhouse and sat at my locker. The tears came. I wasn't hitting, and I couldn't pitch. My future had collapsed around me.

When I looked up, Doc was standing at my side. "Don't worry about it, Maury," he said, wrapping his right arm around my shoulders. "You'll make it. No slump lasts forever."

The next day I was back at second base, my pitching

career ended. But I don't regret those awful moments in Hamilton. From Doc Axelson, I learned consideration in handling young players and from my own experience I learned, firsthand, the pain of failure that hits pitchers in a very special way. It helps a manager to know that feeling, which is peculiar to pitchers since so much rides on their shoulders, and to know how to empathize with it.

One of Ted Williams' major problems as a manager was his inability to relinquish any authority to his pitching coach. Ted demanded the same perfection from his pitchers that he had as a .400 hitter with a picture swing. Ted thought he could teach the pitchers without having a coach as an intermediary. There is just no way it can be done.

One of my first moves as a manager would be the acquisition of the best pitching coach that my owner's money could buy. I'd want a Red Adams, a Johnny Sain, a Ron Perranoski, a man who knows how to *coach*. Since I believe pitching to be at least 70 percent of a team's defense, I'd want to entrust that department only to the best.

On my team the pitching coach would have full authority; his word to a pitcher would be law. While a pitching coach doesn't make the final decisions, his suggestions should play a heavy role in the manager's strategy. But with authority goes responsibility. If I were to see a young pitcher of talent who wasn't progressing according to the timetable or if he were to develop bad habits, I would find fault with the pitching coach.

It is the coach who knows better than anyone when a pitcher is faltering. And it's the coach who goes out to the mound for the conference that determines whether or not the pitcher has the stuff to continue in the game. Only the coach is close enough to the pitcher to tell at a glance if he's off form. He is the vital link between the manager and the pitching staff. This may sound elementary, but I've known managers who had selected unsatisfactory pitching coaches, didn't trust their judgment, or didn't know how to accept sound advice when it was offered. It's impossible to overrate the contributions of an able pitching coach.

Aside from listening to his coach, how does a manager know when a pitcher should be relieved? By intuition, instinct, gut feeling, and one rule: You take the pitcher out of the game when he begins to struggle, not after he's been struggling.

By struggling I mean throwing just a few too many balls. He may get the batter out, but it's an obvious struggle—it's ball one, ball two, foul ball, ball three, foul ball, the count's three and two. Finally, the batter's out of there, but what a struggle! Too many three-and-two counts are a clear sign of struggle.

Once a manager starts hoping his pitcher can get by the next batter, he's going on borrowed time. When confidence goes, hope comes in.

The book says you give the pitcher every chance to complete his ball game. When pitchers do their salary bargaining, one of their selling points is how many games they've completed. I would tell my pitchers not to worry about those completed games—we're more interested in the won and lost column in the standings.

The book also says that you allow the pitcher a chance to make at least one mistake. A mistake means permitting the batter to reach first and another to get on, probably pushing the first one to third. But why wait? When a pitcher has been in some trouble in the seventh and eighth innings, even though the team's ahead, 3–0, why wait until the ninth inning, when he loads the bases, before putting in a relief pitcher? Why wait for him to put even one runner on base? I'd start fresh. Pat the starter on the butt for a good game, and bring the relief pitcher on for the inning.

One of the fundamental responsibilities of the pitching coach is to instruct the pitchers in how to lessen the threat of the base stealers. If you don't stop a Lou Brock, a Joe Morgan, a Davey Lopes, a Cesar Cedeno, they'll run you out of the ball park. The man who must stop them is the pitcher.

A major-league pitcher once told me that he goes by the old theory—the wait system. When there's a speedy runner on first base—a Lou Brock, for instance—he goes to the mound and waits. He tries to outwait the runner, to beat him down with patience. It's a foolish and self-defeating theory. A pitcher can wait forever, but the time must come when he will finally have to commit himself and throw to the plate.

While the pitcher is waiting, the runner's tempo improves as he moves back and forth, but the pitcher becomes increasingly tense. Now the catcher sees the runner stepping out into a big lead, and he calls for a pitchout.

The pitcher throws, but the runner doesn't move. The count is ball one. Since the runner is still off on a big lead, the catcher calls for another pitchout—and still the runner doesn't go. The count is now two balls and no strikes, the catcher must forget about pitchouts—and the runner is in a beautiful spot to steal on the next pitch, which had better be over the plate.

A pitcher can beat this base-stealing play by throwing strikes and throwing fast. All his moves ignore the runner on first. Don't even glance his way. The base runner does not set himself to steal until the pitcher glances over. Instead of that first pitchout, if he throws a strike and the batter takes it, expecting the runner to go, then the pitcher has the advantage both ways.

Let him wing over another quick strike, and the batter is in a bind—he has to start swinging. And even if he hits the next pitch, the runner has lost his opportunity to steal. The more times the pitcher throws to a batter, the greater are the chances for the runner to go. On a three-and-one count, for instance, there's no chance for a pitcher.

The waiting and the fidgeting are sure ways for a pitcher to lose the aggressive base stealer. This may sound obvious. There are few secrets in baseball. But it's also true that remarkably few pitchers know how to handle a good base stealer. So few pitchers know how to vary their rhythm, confront the runner with the unexpected and upset his concentration.

The first baseman has always played the runner close, and that inevitably leaves a gaping hole between first and second—the perfect opening for the hit and run. But that's a part of the baseball book, and it's never questioned.

The truth is that the first baseman gains nothing by hanging close to the base. On the contrary, it's a help to the good base stealer. A Lou Brock, with his sharp peripheral vision, sees the first baseman out of the corner of his eye, and that serves as a guideline to determine the extent of his lead.

On my ball club, with a base-stealing threat on base, the first baseman would stand directly behind the runner about eight feet from the base. If the runner is no threat to steal, I'd want the first baseman still to play eight feet behind him and even deeper. This puts the first baseman in a better position to field a ball hit in that area, which means that it might cancel out the hit-and-run attempt. He can still duck and get to the base if the pitcher wants to go for the pickoff. And if the runner decides to try a ten-foot lead, he has to end up as a dead duck with the catcher shooting a sign to the pitcher, the first baseman, the second baseman, and the shortstop.

It's an effective move to have the first baseman out of the runner's range of vision. Now the runner is saying to himself: "Where the hell is he?" He gets leery, and doubts creep into his mind. Once I remember a first baseman positioned himself in a direct line to my right, assuming that he would be blocking my path toward second base. I had to do nothing more than take one step backward and slip around him. That's about as adventurous as first basemen get.

In establishing pitching as the heart of the defense, I would make it a policy to forget about pregame meetings. They are almost always a waste of time. Throughout my career, from Hornell, New York, and in all the way-stops in the minors and majors, I have heard managers at clubhouse meetings saying, "Jam him." Name a hitter, and the guy says, "Jam him. Pitch to his wrists." I would like to have a dollar for every time I heard Harry "The Hat" Walker say in a Pirates clubhouse meeting, "Jam the son of a bitch!"

The meetings are where the names on the opposing lineup are read aloud, and a manager or a coach is standing up there, saying, "Pitch him high and tight. Pitch this next guy low and away. The guy here is a

good fastball hitter. Keep it tight. This guy likes breaking stuff. Give him fastballs. You gotta keep these guys
honest. Okay, now let's get 'em."

All words from the book—and they are boring,
meaningless, and ineffective. A pitcher can't change
his pattern just because a batter has certain strengths
and weaknesses. Maybe it's just as well for a pitcher to
challenge the hitter, to match his strength against the
batter's strength. As a general rule, the aces of a pitching staff can go against any type of ball club. Tom
Seaver and Bob Gibson are fastball pitchers. But I'd
put Seaver or Gibson up against any fastball-hitting
team.

Against the St. Louis Cardinals, with such good
off-speed hitters as Joe Torre, Lou Brock, and Ted
Simmons, I'd prefer a fastball thrower, but if my ace
happened to be an off-speed pitcher, I'd still go with
him. No matter what the book says, you have to go
with your aces.

More important than how a pitcher throws to certain
hitters is where the fielders are going to play. Consider
this situation: Bud Harrelson of the Mets, a switch-hitter, is batting left-handed against Andy Messersmith
of the Dodgers, a right-hander. Now Harrelson has no
business hitting down the right-field line. Therefore,
he should be played to hit to the left side. And Messersmith must throw fastballs and hard sliders. If he
elects to throw a change-up, a slow-breaking curve,
then the sign should be relayed to the fielders. If a
team is going to have a pregame meeting, positioning
should be discussed instead of pitching. You adjust
your team to emphasize a pitcher's strengths.

In putting together a staff of pitchers, I wouldn't
necessarily demand a bunch of hard-throwing strike-

out artists. The Yankees have done well without a Nolan Ryan or a Tom Seaver or a Sandy Koufax. But I
would want the proper combination—a right-hander
and a left-hander for my aces, another top right-hander
and a top left-hander in the bullpen, a Jim Brewer, a
Mike Marshall, a John Miller.

There is a type of pitcher that I know wouldn't last
on my ball club—the ones who make the first few innings of the game into a bold adventure. These are the
pitchers who wreck your bullpen. They throw too
many pitches, and they're always flirting with trouble
from the first inning. Out in the bullpen, the relief
pitchers are going up and down as the starter never
quite reaches a point of consistency.

Before the game is half over, the bullpen pitchers
have practically thrown nine innings out there. The re-
lievers are ruined, and so is my stomach.

Pitchers must be taught the rudiments of fielding,
especially bunts. We played against Warren Spahn
when he was in the twilight of his career but still blis-
tering fastballs by the hitters. For six innings, Spahnie
was breezing along with a six-hitter. The Braves were
ahead, 2–1, but even that one-run lead seemed comfortable the way he was pitching. Acting as team captain, I called the Dodgers together in the dugout.

"Hey, that old man can stand out there all week and
throw it past us," I said. "Let's break the old bastard's
rhythm. Let's make him field some bunts."

We started bunting, one after the other. In less than
two innings, we had Spahn out of there with bunts that
he couldn't field, and we went on to win.

I suppose it shouldn't surprise anyone that good
fielding pitchers are so rare. Pitchers won't work at
their fielding. All that pitchers ever think about, aside

from hitting home runs in batting practice, are the mechanics of throwing.

Pitching is the most intricate art in baseball, the most demanding and the most all-consuming, physically and emotionally. I accept that. But I'd tell my pitching coach to work at length with the pitchers on their fielding.

I would never use a pitcher as a pinch runner. Too often a manager looks down the bench for a fast runner, and he sees a pitcher with some speed afoot. He sends him in—and risks a career.

Whenever possible, I'd want my pitchers off the base paths. Once in a game in Milwaukee, Sandy Koufax was at second base after a walk and a sacrifice. On a pickoff attempt, Sandy dove back into the base headfirst and fell, with the weight on the inside of his elbow. He stumbled briefly, but he went on to pitch a great game.

A few weeks later the elbow began to flare up. Sandy once told me that he remembered that play at second base so well because the elbow ailment that led to his premature retirement started at that moment.

The theory behind a manager using a pitcher as a pinch runner in, say, the seventh inning is that he doesn't want to use his reserves because he might need them in the fifteenth inning. Or the twenty-seventh. So he takes a chance with a pitcher, usually young and at the start of his career.

Pitchers are the least athletic of all ballplayers and the ones most prone to injury. They should be treated with care. Unless you have a pitcher who can swat the ball, such as a Don Drysdale or a Ferguson Jenkins or a Kenny Holtzman, I'd have my pitcher put down a sacrifice bunt, if it's needed, or give him the take sign. Take every pitch. Forget those big dreams of glory in the batting cage. Let him strike out on called pitches. His job is throwing, not batting. Bill Singer, when he was with the Dodgers, took a swing at an inside pitch, which nipped him on the fingers. He was lost for the rest of the year.

I've known left-handed pitchers who would normally bat right-handed to hit from the left side to protect their pitching arm against the possibility of being hit. That is not a bad idea. On the other hand, I would not force my pitchers to be switch-hitters. Batting from the unnatural side slows the reactions a split second, and the danger of being hit is increased.

All too often, however, managers go beyond the necessary pampering into the area of laxity with their pitchers. They don't bear down on them as they do on the other ballplayers. If a catcher drops four pitches out of fifteen, the manager will take him out of there as fast as he can call for a replacement. How many ground balls can a shortstop afford to miss? Not more than two out of twenty, or else he'd better not send out his laundry. If an outfielder gets twenty fly balls, he had better catch them all.

But the margin of error goes up for pitchers, and I think it can be a calamitous mistake. A major-league pitcher making $50,000 a year should be expected to throw a ball 60 feet 6 inches over a plate that measures 17 inches with a high degree of accuracy.

One reason that a pitcher commits more bases on balls than he should is that he's trying to be a spot thrower. He's out to hit what's called the black of the plate, around the edges. And he can't make it.

Before any pitcher starts throwing for spots, he had better convince me as the manager that he can throw the ball in the strike zone at any given time. He should be able to throw 115 pitches with nearly all of them in the strike zone, or he has no business wearing a major-league uniform.

A pitcher should learn control in spring training. First, we would draw a line down the middle of the plate, and then the pitchers would start throwing—first going for the left side of the plate and then the right side. When that skill is mastered, we cut the plate in half the other way, to form four squares. Then it's up to the pitcher to demonstrate that he can throw to any of the squares designated.

Until a pitcher can throw with that kind of consistency, it's pointless for a catcher to put up his mitt as a location target because the pitcher isn't about to hit it anyway. And the catchers should know when and how to set up a location for the pitcher. As a broadcaster on the NBC telecasts I've seen the center-field camera pick up inexcusable errors in judgment by catchers. With a weak-hitting pitcher at bat, they will give the sign and then hold up a mitt for a location on one corner of the plate. For a weak-hitting pitcher! Then the pitcher on the mound nods and takes aim for the corner, and he misses, and he's committed the unforgivable sin—he's walked the opposing pitcher.

It is a fact, as well as a legend, that pitchers tend to be a breed apart. I've never heard anyone say of a third baseman or a shortstop, "He's a good athlete." But when a pitcher is considered a good athlete, it's a big upset, and they point him out as exceptional.

Some of the most distinctive and colorful pitchers ended up in Dodger uniforms. Just before my time with the club, for instance, there was Billy Loes, a left-hander who would be picked on anybody's all-flake team. Once, in a World Series game, Billy threw a wild pitch and the batter went on to second base.

Afterward Billy was asked what happened. "Oh, I had too much spit on the ball," Billy replied.

In the same game a grounder went through his legs. Billy had an explanation for that: "I lost it in the sun."

Billy Loes was an original thinker. When his career was ended, he tried to catch on with the Brooklyn Dodgers as a batting coach. His theory was that a pitcher would know better than anyone the weaknesses that a hitter should avoid. But he didn't get the job.

On the Los Angeles Dodgers we had a left-hander named Nick Willhite who saw life through his own peculiar tilt. We were playing an exhibition game in Mesa, Arizona, one spring and a writer was interviewing Nick. He was looking for a story that showed some of Willhite's eccentric ways.

"You're talking to the wrong man," Nick insisted. "I'm no different from anyone else."

A few minutes later the national anthem was being played on the loudspeaker. In the ball park at Mesa the flag flies from a pole in the stands behind home plate instead of in the usual spot out past the bleachers. But when the music began, Willhite leaped to his feet, put his right hand on his heart—and stared throughout the national anthem at the center field stands. Everyone in the ball park was looking at the flag except Nick Willhite.

And it was Nick who once threw a pitch that hit his catcher, Jeff Torborg, on the mask.

Jeff got up and hollered, "What the hell are you doing? I haven't even given the sign yet."

"Oh," said Nick, "my rhythm was going so good I didn't want to lose it!"

It must have been Nick Willhite who once put a goldfish in the visiting club's water cooler. Or it could have been Johnny Podres, another Dodger left-hander.

Johnny's main peculiarity was that he never wanted to finish a ball game. He was always anxious to get to a bar and hoist a few. Even if he was doing well, by the seventh inning Johnny would start glancing over at the bench, trying to get the manager's eye. Finally, Walt Alston would walk out to the mound.

"I feel terrible, Skip. Take me out."

Alston had no choice. He'd yank Podres, who would then go in for a quick shower and a rubdown and then look for entertainment. He was a hell of a pitcher, but he wanted to pitch only seven innings.

We also had a pitcher on the Dodgers named Stan Williams, whose nickname was The Big Hurt. Stan was always grabbing people by the neck or the arms, and he could hurt you. He was big and powerful, and he'd come up to a teammate from behind, the way kids do, and put a half Nelson on him until he screamed for help. Stan was a playful kind of guy, and he surprised everybody by turning into a good solid manager in the Boston Red Sox system. Nobody knew that Stan was all that interested in the game. While the other players were sitting around talking strategy, Stan was usually in a corner practicing how to write his autograph for the kids.

"An autograph isn't just a signature," Stan used to say. "An autograph has to have some style!"

Pitchers are always the most superstitious players on a ball club. Let a pitcher win a ball game, and the next time out he'll be wearing the same dirty socks to bring him luck. And don't ever ask a pitcher to lend you his glove. A mother hen is no more possessive of her chicks than a pitcher is of his glove. Let anyone touch his glove, and if the pitcher loses a ball game, he'll think he's been hexed.

Don Sutton has a superstition that I learned about the hard way. As a player I was always trying for the smallest edge. I had one small tactic that I used whenever possible. If I caught an infield fly for the last out or handled the ball on a force-out at second base, I'd take the ball and roll it some distance away from the mound. The opposing pitcher would then have to take a few extra steps and bend over to pick up the ball. I figured that in the heat of August and September, a few extra steps might take away an ounce of energy.

At the same time I always wanted to save our pitcher from any needless bending over. When we took the field, I would rush out and pick up the ball and flip it gently to him as he reached the mound.

Once, when Don Sutton was pitching, I ran out to pick up the ball for him. Just as I was about to grab it, Sutton yelled out, "Don't touch it! Don't touch that ball!"

"What's wrong with it?"

"Just don't touch the ball," Sutton said.

He was serious. He reached over and picked up the ball himself. Sutton believed that unless he were the first to touch the ball as we went on the field, terrible things would happen.

To help out the pitcher, the defense must know what to do in every situation and minimize mistakes. The first rule I would apply is: Forget those long throws from the outfield. This wouldn't necessarily apply to the guns. By a gun, I mean a Willie Mays in his prime, a Willie Stargell today, outfielders with unusually strong arms. There aren't many guns in baseball.

Outfielders delight in making long throws. There's a touch of glamor in throwing the ball into the strike zone and the crowd goes, "Ooooh, what an arm!" As great as he was, Roberto Clemente threw too many long balls instead of depending on a cutoff man. Now the book calls for the outfielders to throw the ball in low and the book is correct—but how many outfielders can execute the play with consistent skill?

For most of the outfielders, the long throw becomes the looping heave, and the runner is thereby given an extra step or two. Notice even in a major-league game how often the throw from the outfield arches in over the cutoff man's glove. How often? From observation, I'd say at least 80 percent of the time.

Two sharp throws, from outfielder to cutoff man to catcher, will usually provide more velocity and much more accuracy. A classic example of this occurred during the 1974 World Series, when Billy Buckner of the Dodgers, running overaggressively, attempted to turn a single and an outfield error by Bill North into a triple. Reggie Jackson, backing up North, picked up the ball and threw a perfect strike to second baseman Dick Green, who in turn whipped another perfect strike to Sal Bando at third, and Buckner was out. The play suffocated what could have been the start of a Dodger rally. The Dodgers went on to lose the game and the Series.

In the years when he was going at full speed, Willie Mays would pull a great play in regard to cutoff throws. Willie is on first, and the next batter hits one to deep center. Willie tears around second and goes to third. Meanwhile, the runner at first has rounded the base and made a slightly threatening move toward second. The outfielder has been forced to go deep, hesitates a split second, and then throws to second. He gives that throw his maximum effort.

In the meantime, Willie has scampered on home, and the other runner has turned around and remained safely at first. But where was the shortstop? Where was the second baseman? Why didn't one or the other run at least thirty feet into the outfield to take a cutoff? Then he would have had the option of throwing to home or to second base.

It never happened. But nobody ever complained, and for this reason—the outfielder threw the ball in low, didn't he? He went by the book, and he might well have blown the game.

The alert manager can be a major bulwark in the defense. Once I saw Gene Mauch work a slick maneuver in defensing bunts. With one out, runners at first and second and a weak-hitting pitcher at the plate, it was an obvious bunting situation. Mauch brought in one of his outfielders to form a five-man infield.

It was a gamble, but it worked. The pitcher, gripping his bat tightly, took one hungry look at that vacant spot in left field, and instead of bunting, he tried to slug the ball. What he hit was a weak grounder to the infield, and that set up the double play. Since Mauch introduced the play, it's been used occasionally by other managers. It's a play that can succeed, however, only with a pitcher who's aware of the dangers involved.

When Frank Lucchesi was managing the Phils, he came up with a defensive play that was even more ingenious. In the seventh inning he had a left-handed pitcher going against a right-handed hitter. Two left-handed hitters were next in the order. Lucchesi called time.

Then he brought in a right-handed pitcher and his lefty out to patrol left field. On the Dodger bench we laughed ourselves silly. What was a pitcher doing out in left field?

But Lucchesi had the last laugh. His right-handed reliever got the left-handed batter out on strikes. Then he was taken out of the game. Now the lefty was brought back in from the outfield—and a substitute replaced him in left—and he handled the next two left-handed hitters, and the inning was over.

I laughed, but I learned. When I was managing winter ball in Mexico, I pulled the same stunt in a similar situation, and they all thought I was a mastermind.

"No," I told them, "the full credit goes to Señor Lucchesi." And I learned not to laugh too quickly.

The manager can't do the playing for his team. A manager can teach, but he can't execute. For instance, I would want my infielders to know how to handle a situation where, say, Lou Brock is on first with one out and Joe Torre hits a fly ball into shortstop territory. I would want my shortstop to know that the prime objective is to get the faster runner, Brock, off the base paths.

What the shortstop must do is let the ball touch his glove and then allow it to drop to the ground. When Brock takes off, we get him. It's not a force-out. The runner must be tagged, but when that is accomplished, we have Brock out of there.

I would also want my infielders to know that with one or two runners on base, not every ground ball is meant to result in a double play. I've seen too many infielders, with double plays in their eyes, charge a ball and miss. I've seen them rush their throws to first and miss there, too, and the runner gets an extra base. The secret is to remain calm and go for the possible.

The defense must do the little things, do them steadily and not yield to pressure. It is the best way I know of to stop a team from stealing a pennant.

5

The Team That Can Steal a Pennant

NONE of my theories works without personnel. And so I have chosen a team that can apply them and steal a pennant. I would want a combination of speed and power—it is difficult to win without at least some power in your lineup. But all too often, I've seen managers get power in a club, and then they forget about speed, and they don't win. You have got to have the proper blend, like a good, crisp salad.

If a manager were to inherit the managership of the Oakland A's, he would be expected to win. If he couldn't win with all that developed talent on his club, what team in baseball will he win with? Instead, what I have elected to do is select a team from today's major leaguers who are best fitted to aggressive offense and preventing aggression while on defense.

But by my own rules in this particular game I want to avoid the obvious. This isn't a team like the A's, loaded with obvious talent all down the line. With only one exception—and that's Bake McBride of the St. Louis Cardinals, a terrific prospect—I have tried to pick players who fall into the same general category. They are players who aren't playing up to their potential usually because they aren't being motivated. Most of them are playing mechanical baseball, and if you asked them, they wouldn't know why. They have talent, they are wearing major-league uniforms, but they are just going through the motions.

I'd like to have the opportunity to mold this group of assorted individuals from both leagues into a team. I think it could be done. It would be fun to try.

Here they are, in the batting order that I would put down on my card:

Bake McBride, rf. Speed is what I want first from a leadoff hitter. Speed like Lou Brock of the Cardinals or Davey Lopes of the Dodgers. I want a man that the opposition has to keep off the base paths because if they don't he'll steal 'em blind. In order to get on and take advantage of this speed he should be capable of 200 hits a year and have the patience to accumulate a lot of walks. He should have an excellent idea of the strike zone.

I want a leadoff man who truly knows how to bunt. If he can bunt and run, it should help him reach that 200-hit mark. I don't want to be too selfish, but I also want the threat of power. McBride also fulfills all these needs. Bake is the kind of player who keeps the pitchers off-balance. He can wait out a walk if the pitcher is unsteady, he can drill a hard single through the infield or beat out a bunt, or he can belt one out of the park.

Many teams have led-off with a light hitter who was a fast runner. But you can't steal first. McBride is a versatile hitter, and along with speed, versatility is what you need here. McBride has burning speed, and he swings a healthy bat. And he fields well. He is the model lead off hitter.

Bud Harrelson, ss. The No. 2 man can be the weakest hitter on the club, but he had better know how to bunt with dependable, unfailing skill. I believe the first two hitters in a lineup set the style for the entire batting order. They are players who can jump on the pitcher, get a runner to second base, and, with the best long-ball hitters on the club up next, take control of the game away from him.

Confidence at bat is one of the prime ingredients I would demand in my No. 2 hitter. He must feel confident he can get a hit no matter what the count since a large part of his job is taking two strikes to give the lead off man a chance to steal. He has to have a feel for the precise dimensions of the strike zone, and he has to be able to put solid wood on the ball on a hit-and-run play.

Jim Gilliam, on the Dodgers of my era, was just about perfect in knowing exactly what to do when a runner was on base. Ted Sizemore fulfilled the same function for Lou Brock in the 1974 season.

I would want speed in my No. 2 man. If the first batter makes out, No. 2 should be able to step into the first hitter's role of getting on base somehow and then become a threat to steal. And he must have the speed to enable him to beat out the bunt.

With the New York Mets, Harrelson bats in the lead-off position, which does not put him in a position to maximize his skills. He doesn't get on base a high percentage of times. I'll assume that McBride will get on base. Then I expect Harrelson to lay down a picture bunt. He might beat it out to first, or it might be a sacrifice. I'd have Bud Harrelson leading the league in sacrifice bunts. He has good speed, and you could bet that he might beat out more than a few of those attempts.

Bud is an outstanding shortstop, but he should develop into more of an offensive threat by learning to bunt expertly and how to punch the ball through the infield. This is crucial. Over the years, if a player's hitting doesn't improve, his defensive ability tends to falter, too. Let Bud Harrelson continue hitting at a .230 clip, and in time his fielding will begin to slip.

One reason that Harrelson stays hurt so much is that he doesn't have enough to keep him motivated. It's hitting, not defense, that keeps a player motivated. Hitting is the heart of baseball. Who ever heard of a gloveman driving a Cadillac?

Bobby Tolan, cf. It should be apparent that the primary job of the third hitter is to move the first and second batters around the bases—all the way is preferred. Willie Mays was, of course, the ultimate third hitter. He had all the assets necessary for the leadoff man and everything you would want your cleanup hitter to have, too. And Willie had the speed that the third hitter must have.

The ideal situation is to fill a lineup with players who have some of the skills of the leadoff man. When you have that going for you, every man up and down the lineup can attack the pitcher and spark a rally.

Bobby Tolan can run, and he can drive in runs with a strong bat. I first remember seeing Bobby when he was with the Jacksonville, Florida, club of the Sally League. I was with the Dodgers then, and we were playing Jacksonville in an exhibition game. I managed to pick Tolan off at second base on a perfect throw from Don Drysdale at the mound. What impressed me then and now is the fact that he was aggressive enough and had the daring to want to go against the Dodgers. I like that. I like aggressiveness wherever I see it.

Here was a minor-league kid challenging us. We all

remembered him on the Dodgers, and we talked about him, knowing that he wasn't long for the Sally League. We could tell from that one game that here was a ballplayer with some drive.

Bobby had some fine years with the Cincinnati Reds until he got into a personality conflict with the front office and was traded to the San Diego Padres, where he hasn't played nearly as well as he should, even allowing for a rash of injuries. Bobby's a good hitter and a good fielder, and he can steal bases. He's still capable of playing major-league baseball on the top level. But Bobby needs a fire built under him.

It's a sound baseball adage that a defensive team must be strong up the middle—catcher, shortstop, center fielder. The reason is borne out in the statistics. They are the players who handle the most chances. They are also the ones who can cut off balls that would otherwise be extra-base hits. As center fielder and shortstop, Tolan and Harrelson would be a perfect combination. Their speed and quickness would close up the holes and make the field seem a lot smaller to the opposing hitter.

Nate Colbert, 1b. If it's necessary to sacrifice speed for power anywhere in the lineup, it should be in the cleanup spot, which is aptly named. You want a hitter who can clean up the bases. The first three spots are occupied by high percentage hitters. Now, in the fourth spot, you need someone who invariably puts mean wood on the ball.

I'm not necessarily interested in the player with the highest batting average on the club going in at cleanup. Consider Johnny Bench, who may not hit .300, but

if he keeps getting those runs batted in—around 100 a
year—then the batting average is secondary.

I like Nate Colbert. I like the way he hits the ball.
But I also like the fact that he provides the added luxury of being able to run. On a ball club where the style
is aggressiveness, I would want my cleanup hitter to
steal some bases even if he isn't gifted with outstanding speed. With the Dodgers of the fifties and sixties,
even Duke Snider, a long-ball hitter, stole a few bases.

Nate emerged in the early 1970s as one of the top hitters in baseball. One night against Atlanta he poled
five home runs and drove in thirteen runs in a doubleheader. But now you mention the name, and in reply
you get a "Nate who?" When Willie McCovey was acquired by the San Francisco Giants, Nate was moved
to the outfield. But that by all rights shouldn't have
had any measurable affect on him. Something happened to Nate in his last year or two with the Padres
before he was traded to Detroit. Somewhere he lost his
concentration and his desire to be recognized as a great
home run hitter. Nate even put on weight and lost a
step or two from the speed that once made him one of
the fast runners in the National League.

Nate, above all, needs motivation and reassurance
that he's still a fine major-league ballplayer. His best
years should be ahead of him, but someone must instill confidence in him so that he plays the game with
the approach that he once had. Nate Colbert still has
the ability to lead any league in home runs and runs
batted in and be a threat on the bases. A remodeled
Nate Colbert could still help any team steal a pennant.

I have known of teams that sacrifice fielding at first
base in favor of added power, but it is not something

that I would recommend. On my kind of team I would want a first baseman along the lines of Wes Parker or Bill White, both slick fielders who could make the big play and keep runners off the base paths. An erratic fielding first baseman tends to put unnecessary pressure on the infielders, who feel that they must always come through with a perfect throw on every play.

Nate Colbert happens to be a big man, but size, contrary to the book, is not a requisite for a first baseman—not on my ball club. It is a curious thing about first basemen. For years, it was believed that first basemen should be left-handed. According to the theory, the left-handed first baseman had his glove hand away from the baseline and was, therefore, in a better position to field balls hit to right. A left-handed first baseman also looked more graceful. Then, in time, right-handed first basemen were accepted. But the old book rule still holds on size—a first baseman must be tall. That, I have always contended, is a fallacy, and for the best of evidence I point to Steve Garvey of the Los Angeles Dodgers, who stands under six feet and knows few equals in fielding his position.

Every so often in a ball game a tall first baseman will make a great play, stretching all the way to nail down an errant throw from the infield. "And that's why you need a tall man at first base," baseball's followers of the book will tell you. To that kind of unimaginative thinking, I reply that nearly all the throws to first base go to the baseman somewhere between the waist and the shoulders and are, as a result, easily caught by the smaller player. A major-league infielder shouldn't be throwing the ball anywhere else—and the few throws that would elude him because of his size are better than having some big guy out there who's sluggish afield. I would prefer the smaller player who can cover the ground and handle bunts. I'm only five feet ten, stretched, but I know I could cover first base better than a number of the slow-footed, clumsy big men I've seen over the years.

Lou Piniella, cf. To me, a batting order is very similar to a pyramid of power, with the fourth and fifth hitters forming the peak. Naturally, I wouldn't turn down any home run hitters, but you have to remember that even the best home run sluggers today only hit about thirty a year which is less than one in every five games. So it must be assumed that the fifth hitter, whether or not he's capable of those thirty home runs a year will be at bat with men on base. In that respect, he has much in common with the cleanup man. Like the cleanup man, the fifth hitter must be able to make contact with the ball with a high degree of frequency. The fifth hitter should not be a player who's victimized into too many strikeouts.

My man for that vital spot is Lou Piniella, who is an excellent hitter. I suspect that Lou has never been happy in his major-league career, first with the Seattle Pilots, then with Kansas City and then the Yankees. His attitude has never been what it should be. But if Lou were to be put into a good frame of mind, he has the ability to lead the league in hitting. As a fielder he would be graded as adequate to good. But I think that could be upgraded, too, if Lou had the confidence of a manager and if he felt that he weren't on trial in every game. That kind of pressure is destructive to a ballplayer. Lou deserves a better shot at the stardom that could be his under other circumstances.

* * *

Gene Tenace, c. To my way of thinking, a lineup is made up of two distinct parts. There are the hitters who go from the leadoff to fifth slots in one part, and the sixth through ninth form the other. Very few ball clubs have four power hitters spread throughout a lineup. The Dodgers can offer Bill Buckner, Steve Garvey, Ron Cey, and Joe Ferguson. With the Oakland A's it's Joe Rudi, Reggie Jackson, Sal Bando, and Gene Tenace. But these are past champions of the National and American Leagues, and they are a rarity.

In my lineup, I see the first through fifth hitters as a blend of speed and power, with each of the players setting the next up for the kill. In the second part of the batting order, beginning with the sixth hitter, you don't expect power behind them, and the trick is to scrap for runs.

The ideal combination of hitters to bat sixth, seventh, and eighth would be composed of players who are, in terms of style, leadoff and No. 2 type hitters. They must be ballplayers who can bunt with skill, steal bases, and generate one run at a time. They are players capable of maintaining the pressure on the pitcher, giving him no opportunities to coast. Gene Tenace fills the bill admirably for the sixth slot. He's fast enough, he can drop a bunt, and he can come through with a home run with runners on base.

Catching is one of the more difficult arts in baseball. The average catcher can handle pitches thrown to the strike zone. But the good catcher is one who blocks balls in the dirt, especially with runners on base. I like a catcher who can throw well enough to catch a good base stealer, provided the pitcher does his job. Accuracy is a must. And I like a catcher who can squat into position low enough so that he doesn't block the umpire's vision—it's hard enough for the average umpire to keep his eyes fixed on the plate.

Mostly, I like a catcher who can handle pitchers. A good catcher is also a good psychologist. He knows his pitchers as human beings; he knows their quirks and idiosyncrasies, and most pitchers have them. A good catcher knows how to anticipate what his pitcher wants to throw, and a good catcher knows when to give the sign that surprises the opposition. A good catcher knows how to win the confidence of his staff, and that means he must have qualities of leadership.

In my time with the Dodgers, John Roseboro had all these qualities in full measure. John could field his position with the best; he could block the plate against a runner coming home; he could handle pitchers; he could nip the base stealers; he was constantly alert.

As his roommate I can say that John Roseboro had only one flaw—he had a tin ear. No appreciation for music whatsoever. How else can I explain the fact that he didn't like my banjo playing? But I had to forgive him for that one lapse when he put on the mask and chest protector.

Joe Torre was another catcher I admired. Although Joe had what I would judge as the weakest arm in the National League, for me he was just about the toughest of all the catchers to steal on. Joe had an astonishingly quick release and great accuracy. Perhaps another way of putting it is to say that Joe Torre was a baseball player first and then he was a catcher.

Ted Sizemore, 2b. Here's the pivotal hitter in the second half of my lineup. He's the man who helps produce runs because he has intelligence, as well as the necessary baseball skills. Sizemore is one of the best second-spot hitters in the game, and as my seventh batter he fulfills the same function in the bottom of the lineup. In 1974 he lost some points in his batting average, but in a real sense he protected Lou Brock on the base paths and enabled Brock to break my base-stealing record.

Sizemore is also my team captain, a scrappy, wily, clever Eddie Stanky type of player. By that I mean that Sizemore possesses no outstanding tools—no great power or great arm or great speed, but all these attributes are good enough, and he has a superlative winning attitude. As a Dodger, Ted was rookie of the year, giving promise then of the type of major-league ballplayer he would become with maturity. Mentally, Ted is a sharp athlete; he knows the game from the inside. I also like him because he's a solid and dependable bunter.

Billy Grabarkewitz, 3b. The eighth hitter operates like the No. 3 hitter. He should have the characteristics of a leadoff man who can get on base and then be bunted to second by the pitcher, who follows him in the order. He should also be able to move the sixth and seventh batters around the bases.

According to old baseball theory, the eighth man is the team's weak stick—and he goes to waste. On my ball club the eighth hitter would, among other things, be a specialist in the sacrifice bunt. In a situation where the eighth hitter comes to bat with two outs, on many ball clubs he's considered virtually an automatic out. How much better it is for the eighth man to be able to beat out a bunt or punch out a single. Then the pitcher bunts him over, and we have something going. We're keeping the pressure on the opposing pitcher.

Billy Grabarkewitz came up to the Dodgers in the early seventies, and he had a fantastic rookie year. At the start everyone was asking, "Is Grabby for real?" Then he was injured, and he didn't play much after that. In fact, he never played enough with the Dodgers. He was traded to the Angels and then to the Phils, where I thought manager Danny Ozark would provide the spark to bring back his self-confidence. But that didn't happen, and Grabby was dealt to the Cubs, where he was wasted.

All that ability, and so little is being done with it. Now that Bill is more mature, it seems to me he should be a super ballplayer. For my club to have him would be a steal.

It is part of the baseball book, incidentally, that a third baseman should have the strongest arm in the infield. I disagree. In the latter stages of my career, I moved from shortstop to third base, which I had always considered the old folks' home. I learned otherwise. A batted ball tends to take a different kind of hop when it's hit toward third, and the ex-shortstop or ex-second baseman had better learn to adjust. Some old folks' home! However, I also learned that since a ball hit to third usually has more velocity—the hot-corner label is no myth!—the third baseman has more time to make his play, and for that reason he doesn't need a rifle for an arm. An average throwing infielder can fill the bill at third. The strongest arm is needed by the shortstop. But the second baseman should have nearly as good an arm. He must field any number of chances hit to his right, which usually require a long, hard throw. A weak-armed second baseman has no future.

One day another myth will fall when the time-honored restriction is lifted against left-handers at second base, shortstop, and third base. And for that matter, outside of the absurd fact that sporting goods manufacturers don't turn out left-handed mitts, why not a lefty catcher? A left-handed fielder could play any of these positions, make the throws and necessary moves with just as much facility as the right-handers. The left-handers are stopped only by tradition, 105 years of playing by the book.

For pitchers, I would take Jon Matlack of the Mets, Wayne Garland of the Orioles, Ferguson Jenkins of the Red Sox, and Buzz Capra of the Braves.

As far as the fans are concerned, Matlack has been overshadowed by Tom Seaver, but he's a fine pitcher nonetheless. There is much to like about Jon Matlack. He has excellent control, a good breaking pitch, and what ballplayers call a long fastball that moves. He's also blessed with an attribute that you don't always find in pitchers, and that is stamina. He doesn't wear out.

Poise is the one word that comes to mind when I think of Wayne Garland. Although Wayne has an assortment of pitches, his hard fastball is what impresses me the most. He's a pitcher who doesn't nibble around. He charges the batter. I like that quality in a pitcher.

Ferguson Jenkins is a first-rate pitcher who was permitted to get away from the Cubs because they thought he had passed his peak. Not by my yardstick he hasn't. I'd take him for my staff. Unlike the others on this staff, Jenkins has attained his potential, but with proper handling he could add a lot to a pitching corps, which by my definition consists of players who are ready to pitch in rotation every four days.

As for Buzz Capra, I like him for two valid reasons. First, he's an extremely promising pitcher with both control and speed. Second, he's not a big man. And therein lies a theory of mine which goes against the ancient baseball fallacy, one more aspect of the book, which says pitchers should be big. Where is it written in marble that the speed of a thrown ball has any relationship to the size of the body?

It's sheer fallacy that a big man can necessarily throw a ball with greater velocity than a small man. I've seen little men who could throw the ball through a wall. And where is it written that the little men have less stamina than the big hulks? It is sheer visual deception. A big man may look strong and durable, but the little man may well be even stronger and more durable. Size means bulk; it doesn't necessarily indicate strength. You don't measure the capability in a pitching arm by the size of the biceps.

These are pitchers who fulfill my philosophy of what a staff should be. They are pitchers who throw a lot of strikes. I want pitchers who don't allow themselves to become intimidated. And I want pitchers, as these men are, who are baseball-smart, with guile and cunning in their arsenal as well as the fastball, curve, slider, and change-up. I want pitchers who are mean!

What I would never want on a staff are throwers. There are many pitchers in the game today who have to be classified among the throwers—and I might add here that I have never seen a little guy who was ever a thrower. The throwers try to get along on strong arms alone, and of course, some of them do. But they wouldn't do that on my staff. I'd want pitchers who think, who set the hitters up, outsmart them, and embarrass them.

To the above I would want to add one player that I would dearly love to have on my ball club, and that is the controversial Dick Allen. Unlike the others, Dick's talent has always been fully realized. I would just want him around because he does anything asked of him in a ball game. If Dick Allen wanted to sing the national anthem before a game, I'm sure he could do it—and he'd know all the lyrics, too.

Allen is the best combination of speed, power, and percentage hitting in baseball today. He could be placed anywhere in the lineup and fill all the requirements. I can think of only two other ballplayers today who come close, and they are Bobby Bonds of the Angels and Jimmy Wynn of the Braves.

As I have previously indicated, each player on a club must be treated differently, making allowances for individuality. I contend that for a Dick Allen, with his natural gifts, a manager must make special rules. I don't mind dealing with sensitive ballplayers. I was one myself.

Dick Allen could be anything he wanted to be on my ball club, including the designated hitter if that were to his liking. The notion of a designated hitter is a new blessing that the American League wisely added to the game, and I am heartily in favor. A loosely defined hitter, the designated hitter gives the manager an added luxury, and anything he does can be fitted in to the lineup. A good trader will keep his eyes alert for any player who has the offensive potential to be a designated hitter.

Originally, when the concept of the designated hitter went into effect, managers sought out the power hitters for the job. It was a relative innovation and managers weren't ready to cope with all the possibilities. A designated hitter should be a power hitter or one who has a high average. But on my club, if I had all the other components, I would want speed in my designated hitter.

What could be better than to have one more player available to tantalize the pitcher? How great it would be to have one more player who could move around the bases and give the opposition fits. My mouth positively waters at the thought when I dwell on the possibility of removing the pitcher from the lineup and putting in another pesky little demon on the base paths. If the National League would have had the designated hitter rule in effect at the time, my own major-league career might not have ended so abruptly. And I could have stolen some more bases in the bargain.

That's the ball club that could put my theories of aggressive baseball into play and steal a pennant. It's a club that could make its presence known, and I guarantee it would cause a lot of damage in either league.

Is there a team that could never steal a pennant? There sure is. They are the Atlanta Braves. As a team, with all their good players of major-league caliber, they remind me of the golfer who has the perfect picture swing—the gallery goes "ooh" and "ah" on every stroke—but he never wins a tournament. I am aware of the fact that the Braves won in divisional play in 1969 and then lost in the pennant play-off to the Mets, but it was a sheer fluke that they ever advanced that far.

The Braves simply don't have a winning style. They don't have any of the extras that it takes to win with consistency. It is definitely not what I would term a hustling ball club. So often I've seen Braves pop up to the infield—even to the outfield—and never make it to first base. Playing at home in Atlanta, they will make a right turn from the base path to the Braves' dugout.

This is a club with impressive individual statistics. But it's a team that doesn't know how to make use of its talent. It's a team gone stagnant. The Atlanta Braves are a team that follows the book completely.

6

"You Don't Handle Men—You Handle Horses"

—WILT CHAMBERLAIN

(Dear Wilt: You're Wrong)

GETTING into baseball was a struggle for me from the very beginning as a kid in Washington, D.C. After signing with the Dodger organization fresh out of high school for a whopping $500, I spent eight and a half seasons on what seemed to me an endless and frustrating odyssey through the minor leagues until they finally decided I was ripe for the majors. I was ripe, all right—I was a twenty-seven-year-old rookie, and that made me one of the older players on the club.

Getting out of baseball as a player was much easier. I didn't have to sit through that emotional period, full of doubt and indecision, that hits some players—and some of the great ones, too, such as Hank Aaron. The Dodgers made that decision for me.

I was on the golf course at Los Coyotes in Los Angeles, standing at the fourteenth tee, feeling good about the drive I had just hammered straight down the fairway. Then I noticed several golf carts coming over the hill. I recognized them as reporters and photographers from two Los Angeles television stations. I knew they weren't out there to cover my golf game.

"Hiya, fellas," I said. And waited.

One of them said, "Maury, the Dodgers just announced it. You've been released."

I felt momentarily numb. Then the cameras began to roll, and the questions were asked.

I began by saying, "It's been great being a Dodger. . . ."

And it was. But at that moment when I thought the world was against me, a line that I had heard George Jessel say once at a banquet suddenly flashed through my mind. It went like this: "He who thinks the whole world is against him is overestimating his own importance."

I heard myself saying the "right" things, being a team player even though I was no longer a part of the team. But continuing along that vein would have been just as hypocritical as my saying, as I did a few years later, that records are made to be broken and it's nice that Lou Brock broke mine. Well, it just isn't so.

A year earlier, in 1971, I had been voted the major-league shortstop of the year. Dammit, I remember thinking to myself, I had set a major-league record for this team, I had drawn millions of fans to the ball park. I had won a most valuable player award. I was one of the Dodger stars. I had played my heart out for this team for ten years. And now they close the door on me, and what's more, they tell everyone else in town about it before they tell me.

Once I had a manager in the minors named Ray Hathaway, an easygoing man who used to say to his players, "Have fun, boys. Baseball's a game." It's a great game, but it can be a rotten business.

When I was paired with Sam Snead in the Doral tournament pro-am a few months after the Dodgers released me, we were talking about sport as business. I told Sam that if I could have chosen any professional sport other than baseball, it would have been golf.

Sam nodded. "Nobody can tell you when to retire as a golfer," he said. "Nobody can tell you that you've had it, get off the tour. You have no manager or coaches telling you when to get in for curfew or how much you have to practice. You don't get fined if you miss a shot. Thing is, I don't play for a team. I play for Sam Snead."

That is the heart of the matter. When you're involved in a team sport, they tell you when to leave, and I feel that I was shown the door too early.

I have always believed that a player who has enjoyed a measure of success should go out of the game in the dignity of retirement. But one of the cliches in the book says the player himself is always the last to know.

No, the player is the first to know. He may try to hide that fact from his manager, perhaps even from himself, but he knows. "He hung on too long," they say about a player who is around the bend, a step slower than in his prime. But suppose a star player does hang on for an extra year—one year after he's had a productive season. He's been in the game for, let's say, eighteen or twenty years. He's surely not going to hang on for five more years—one year is all he asks, a year to give the game one last strong effort to prove to himself what his own capabilities are—one year, but not for somebody to decide for him.

Officially, I never retired. I was released. In the next few weeks after being handed my walking papers, my phone bill soared. I placed calls to the White Sox, the A's, the Tigers, the Padres, the Cardinals, the Reds, and a few others.

Three calls were returned. Two were negative. The

other offered hope. The head of one major-league club said to me, "Can you coach third base?"

"Coach? Hell, I can manage a ball club."

"Of course you can. But sometimes coaching is the way to get a foot in the door. The first step. One step at a time. Can you still play? Can you play third base?"

My hopes were lifted. "I can play," I said. "I can coach. I can manage. Name it. I'll do anything. I'll go early to spring training. I'll teach the rookies. I'll give you every last bit of what I know about the game."

The conversation ended, for me at least, on a note of optimism. But for whatever reason—and since he is an honorable man I know it was a reason that seemed valid to him at the time—he never called me back.

Shortly thereafter the offer came from NBC. It was the beginning of a new career, in broadcasting, and I was still where my heart has always been, in baseball. But the question gnaws at me: Is this any way to treat a player, not allowing him the privilege of resigning from the game that he has given so much of his life? Unfortunately, my case is hardly untypical—it happens every year, and it happens to a lot of fine ballplayers—and it is indicative of an attitude. It is always possible for a manager to tell a player personally, in the kindest manner, with some appreciation for his feelings, that he can no longer be a part of the ball club. It is a rocking blow that must be softened with thoughtfulness. And it is just as much a part of handling players as any other aspect of managing a major-league baseball team.

As a black manager I would have to say that the handling of players is inextricably involved today with an understanding of the racial differences. Color is a fact of life. Color can't be ignored, and it shouldn't be magnified, but it must be acknowledged. What matters is the manager's attitude toward color, how he relates personally to the whites, the blacks, and the Latins on his ball club—and today you don't have to be much of an observer to know that on most teams that will be your racial mix in varying degrees. A manager with even a hint of prejudice in him—whether it's a white against blacks or Latins or a black against whites or any combination of bias—has the odds stacked against him.

At home the attitude starts with the parents. On a ball club the manager's attitude creates the prevailing atmosphere. My job as manager would be to establish direct and honest communication with each player, whatever his color. I think that I understand the white ballplayer. Blacks have always made it their business to understand white people. I know something about the sensitivities of black players that come with living and playing in a white man's world.

I know about the ways we used to test white players by offering them a cigarette after we had taken a few puffs—just to see if they would put it to their lips. Or how we would offer a white player a drink we had tasted, and then we'd notice with studied casualness if they would spin the glass around. These were small, perhaps even petty tests, but sensitivities can run deep, and we were always searching for a white give-away that indicated what we would interpret as preju-dice. Put a black in with whites and his instincts, care-fully honed through the years, alert him to any sign of prejudice because that is how blacks have always lived. It goes with the skin pigment.

The entire issue of race in baseball remains compli-cated and a reflection of the world outside baseball. Al-though Jackie Robinson did break the so-called color line, in some ways it's been a long time disappearing. It's a fact that the races are treated differently. For instance, any black player who's been around the game for any length of time knows that he's supposed to play hurt. The late Don Wilson, who pitched for the Houston Astros, put it all in a sentence when he told me privately, "Unless we've got a bone sticking out and we're moaning with pain and hollering for the medics, nobody ever believes we're hurt."

It's a curious double standard to impose on athletes. To hazard a guess about its roots, maybe it comes from the still all-too-widespread feeling that being good at sports comes "natural" to blacks, and therefore, we don't have to work at our skills. And since, according to that theory, it comes so easy to us, nothing short of two broken legs would ever be a handicap on the field.

Well, it simply isn't true. I started out as a good athlete, with good reflexes and sharp eyes, but developing into a major-league baseball player didn't come easy or natural to me. Hitting home runs didn't come any more natural to Hank Aaron than it did to Babe Ruth.

The double standard operates in other subtle ways. Even today there are very few marginal black players in the big leagues. To make it to the majors, a black player doesn't have to be a superstar, but he had better be a top-level ballplayer. What I'm saying is common knowledge, even though it has remained unspoken—the baseball book states that the average black player, generally speaking, has to have more ability to make it to the big leagues than the average white player. Anyone who denies this is simply denying the facts.

I can talk now about how black players should be handled—treated, perhaps, is a better word—because I have my own recollections of how I was treated. This goes back to when the Dodgers chose me to break the ice as the first black player ever to play for their farm club in the Texas League, the Fort Worth Cats. It was 1955, only a year after desegregation had been ruled the law of the land by the Supreme Court, and black players were just beginning to play in what had hitherto been the lily-white leagues in the South and Southwest.

From the start, I could feel a draft, which is an expression blacks use to describe a feeling of prejudice hanging in the air so heavy that you can feel it inside you. I flew into Fort Worth, and I was met at the airport by a representative of the ball club.

"You're Wills," he said.

"Yes, I am," I said.

That was about the extent of our conversation. He looked around furtively to make sure nobody saw him in company with a black man, and then he hustled me off by car to the ball park. Somebody put a pen in my hand to sign the contract, and then they rushed me out. I felt as though I were playing a bit part—a token black role?—in a James Bond spy movie.

This was a quiet Sunday night in Fort Worth. I was driven to a hotel across the street from the train depot and told to check in. Now I've seen small hotel rooms—I had a room once in Amarillo, Texas, that was only big enough for the roaches—but this one wasn't even fit to be called a closet.

There was no ventilation, and the only bathroom was down at the end of the hallway. Sleep was impossible. Outside, through the window, I could see a neon sign blinking on and off. All night I heard the sounds of railroad boxcars moving in and out, and the clanging of train bells. Is this a way to handle any ballplayer, black or white?

I have quite a few memories of mishandling by the

Fort Worth Cats. The next morning I took my first trip with the club, to Shreveport, Louisiana. We arrived late at night, and the bus stopped in front of a hotel. The white players, along with the manager, an old Dodger outfielder named Tommy Holmes, and the coaches, left the bus in a group and went inside.

"Say, where do I go?" I called out to Danny Ozark, who was our first baseman and road secretary and eventually manager of the Philadelphia Phils. "What am I supposed to do?"

Danny stared at me. "I don't know," he said. "Didn't they tell you?"

I shook my head. Now I had become a problem. Danny shrugged and went into the hotel. I'm sure he had his own problems without bothering his head about race relations in the state of Louisiana.

So there were two of us, the trainer, who was black, and me. We stood in front of the hotel, our bags at our feet. I remember only that the trainer's first name was Alex and that he was an older man and he obviously knew his way around the traditions of the South.

We started walking. We walked and walked until we arrived at what was obviously a black section of town. By now it was about one in the morning, and we were exhausted and embittered.

We began knocking on doors, trying to get someone to put us up for the night. Everywhere we went, we would get a puzzled, sleepy glance and a shake of the head and a slamming of the door in our faces.

Finally, an elderly black couple allowed us to sleep on cots on their open back porch. They clicked the back door shut and bolted the lock. We slept fitfully. The next morning we were told, "On your way. We said we'd give you a place to sleep last night. We didn't say we'd feed you."

Now we were getting it from our own people. Welcome to Shreveport!

Beginning with no breakfast, it was a long day in a strange city in the Deep South. By late afternoon we began to look for a cab to go to the ball park for the night game. In Shreveport there was only one black cab—it was against local law for a white cabdriver to pick us up—and by the time we arrived at the ball park, we were a half hour late.

The white players had long since arrived from the white hotel, on the team bus. We were late, and Tommy Holmes wouldn't hear any excuses.

"Where the hell were you guys?" Holmes demanded, glowering at us.

I started to explain. "Never mind," Holmes said. "Get dressed."

Again I tried to explain, but Holmes interrupted me before I could get two words out. "Wills," he said, "this is your first day with the club. The least you could do is be here in time."

Back in Fort Worth, for our first home game, I walked several blocks from my hotel alongside the railroad yards and boarded a public bus to go out to the ball park. I paid my fare, and I saw two players from the team. They were seated behind the driver. I joined them, and we talked briefly.

"Hey, boy!"

I looked up. Then I realized the bus hadn't moved. The driver was standing over me. His eyes were full of red-neck menace.

He pointed to a sign on the wall near the back of the bus. It said: COLORED ONLY.

Slowly, I got up and walked to the back of the bus. It was a long, painful walk. Not that I was unaware of prejudice, but I had previously experienced remarkably little of it. Still, I must have been innocent not to have expected it in the heart of Texas, in the year 1955.

At the ball park the players who had been on the bus were joking about the bus incident, and everybody in the clubhouse roared with laughter. These were my own teammates, and they thought it was hilarious that I had been humiliated in public because of my color.

That summer I bought a car, an ancient clunker with a broken gas gauge. It wasn't much help never knowing how much gas I had in the tank. Besides, the gasoline was always being siphoned out of the tank, and I'd run out of gas and be late for the ball game, and Tommy Holmes would say, "Are you late again, Wills?"

There are other incidents I could recall, none of them any more demeaning than what other black ballplayers have gone through. But I was a Baptist minister's son, with religious training, from a nice home. I had been taught the virtues of brotherly love, and at Fort Worth I was placed in a situation that I couldn't handle. That summer I was often on the bench, burning inside with anger and frustration. I finished with a dismal .202 batting average, the lowest in my career.

I mention this episode in my career as a clear-cut illustration of how a manager's insensitivity and unpleasant surroundings can affect a player. If a man gains in character through pain or adversity, then the season in Fort Worth might be called profitable. I learned from an outrageously bad example that understanding and empathy can be among a manager's most effective tools. It is something I have thought about deeply in assessing my own approach to managing. Ballplayers aren't cogs in a machine that you wind up and send out on a field. They are men with human emotions and problems, and they need your understanding, an attribute that I believe is just as important as knowledge of the game. In other words, a manager should know men as well as he knows baseball.

Times have changed since I first came into baseball, but the unwritten rule in regard to road trips, a time when a player usually shares a hotel room with a teammate, is still that you don't mix the races. When Curt Blefary, who is white, roomed with Don Wilson, a black man, the Astros' management wanted to know what the hell was going on.

"We're buddies; we have similar interests; we just thought we'd room together," Wilson explained. I think the Astro management is still perturbed about it.

It's not unheard-of, but it is a rarity for black and white ballplayers to room together. Pro football mixes up the races on the road, while baseball goes by the old tradition. But tradition can make for restrictions in our thinking. A manager, most of all, can't allow himself to be victimized by meaningless tradition.

As a manager I'd ask my general manager to allow the players to choose their own roommates. Most often, beginning in spring training, the club assigns roommates—usually pitchers go with pitchers, catchers with catchers, and so forth. In time, friendships are formed, and changes may be requested. A pattern usually evolves that's easily predictable. The cardplayers room together; the drinkers room with other drinkers; the TV watchers stick together. Rarely does a single player room with a guy who's married.

Roomies obviously have to have something in common. It's true that many white players would rather not room with a black teammate, and it works the other way, too. A white player from Nebraska who likes Johnny Cash isn't about to share a room happily with a black player from New York who prefers Gladys Knight and the Pips on his tape deck.

On a club of mine, I'd like to see a white and a black player decide to room together. And then maybe a few others would do it, and some of the barriers would come tumbling down. It might also break down some of the cliques that turn up on ball clubs.

The entire issue of race becomes even more complicated when it involves the Latin ballplayers. After living in countries where race really isn't much of an issue, it must puzzle the hell out of the Latins when they come to the United States to play. Take a typical case of two players up from Venezuela. One has kinky hair and dark skin, and here, in the United States, he's considered black. The other has straight hair and a light complexion, and here he's considered white. Back in the days—and not all that long ago, either—when black athletes couldn't eat in the same restaurants with the whites, this presented quite a problem, and it perplexed the Latins.

After they are here for a while, the Latins begin to take on some of our attitudes about social inferiority. The darker Latin players soon become very sensitive about race. For instance, when the Latins who are considered "black" are with other American players, black or white, they will talk reasonably good English. But when they are out in public, the situation changes.

If several "black" Latins are on a hotel elevator with other people around, they'll quickly begin to speak rapid Spanish. It may be that they are more comfortable speaking in their tongue, but I suspect the real reason is that they would rather be considered Latin Americans than black Americans. And this, sadly, is what they learn from us. Some good neighbor policy.

Latins also fall victim to our custom of expecting blacks to play ball whatever the state of their health. For two years, with the Pirates, I played with Roberto Clemente, a great outfielder from Puerto Rico. Clemente was very moody, with emotional ups and downs, and it never helped his moods to read about how Mickey Mantle went out there and played for the Yankees in spite of his injuries.

Roberto would become enraged. He would read an article with reference to Mantle playing hurt, and then he'd squeeze the paper in his powerful hands and hurl it to the floor in disgust. "Hell with them," Roberto would say. "Shove it, Mickey Mantle. I have headaches. I don't sleep nights, my back hurts like fire, but nobody believes me. Even when they do believe me, they still say, 'Oh, you can play, Roberto.' The hell I can. But I do."

It all adds up to one word—prejudice. It happens to be a very interesting word, prejudice. Broken down to its roots, it means prejudging. It means making a judgment before you know what you're judging. It may be a part of human behavior in an imperfect world, but it's still stupid to prejudge people. Prejudice is stupid.

I think I know something about Latin players. When I managed winter ball in 1970 in Hermosillo, Mexico, we won the league championship with a team of fourteen Mexican players and six Americans, two of them black. And what's more I sent four of my players up to the big leagues.

I have heard it said by baseball men, followers of the book, that managing in winter ball doesn't count for much. The hell it doesn't. Managing winter ball in Latin America is just as difficult as—maybe even more difficult than—managing in the big leagues.

You begin with a complex situation. First, the Americans who go down to Mexico are paid as much in expenses as the others are getting in salary, and this is resented by the Mexican players. To an American, often sent there by a parent club, a winter playing ball in Mexico isn't quite a vacation, but he's only there to develop certain phases of his game. To him, this is a proving ground, but to the Mexicans this is their season, and they want results, not some guy working on his slider.

Next, there is the language barrier. The Americans as a rule can't speak Spanish, and the Mexicans have very little English. The American are there throughout the holidays, through Thanksgiving, Christmas, New Year's, and they grow homesick. And there's the food and the altitude, both troublesome for Americans.

I started out with only a few basic words of Spanish at my command. In clubhouse meetings my third base coach was the translator, and I have the feeling a lot was lost in the translations to judge from what would happen later on the field.

Once, after we had lost a doubleheader to an inferior club, I was furious. I was chewing the players out in English and then watching for a reaction as the words were translated into Spanish. I saw no change of expression on the faces of the Latin players. Why weren't they offended or angry? They sat there and nodded. I have to figure that the translation lost something of the sting in my remarks.

That is when I vowed to learn Spanish in the fastest possible crash course. For the next ten days I spoke no English. I kept consulting my grammar book, and I spoke in halting Spanish. But I learned. On the eleventh day, I called a clubhouse meeting, and I addressed the team—in Spanish. I may have had a few tenses wrong, but how the Latin players ate it up.

Suddenly, that team came alive. In time, I had the Mexicans teaching Spanish to the Americans, and the Americans teaching English to the Mexicans—all learned choice examples of profanity first, of course. Soon, in the team bus, the players weren't huddling in groups with their own. They became a team that was fluent—well, fluent enough—in two languages.

A part of managing is knowing when and how to con your players, when to pull the Robert Redford-Paul Newman number. On bus trips through the Mexican countryside, we would stop for lunch in roadside enchilada parlors. Occasionally, I would sit with several Mexican players. I'd tell them, more or less, "Hey, guys, you know these Americans down here are on a kind of vacation, which isn't fair. I told them to forget that vacation crap. I told them that when they play for me, they hustle. They agreed and said they'll play for me as hard as they would at home. So they're going all out now. Meantime, you guys have got to keep going. This is your league. You've got to represent it well and play your best, too." They would nod and agree and go out and hustle.

Now I go back to the Americans. "Hey, guys, you know you can't expect the Mexicans to come up to the brand of ball you play. They're looking for you to lead them and show them how it's done, which is no more than right. Baseball is our game. You guys are representatives of the game of baseball, and you've got to represent it well. Besides, if you do well here you've got a much better shot at the big leagues." They would nod and agree and go out and try to outhustle the Mexicans.

Before each game we had a skull session with the blackboard and then a half hour instructional period. We bunted; we worked pickoff plays; we worked on baserunning, the hit and run. We had a player on the club, Hector Espino, who was the perennial triple crown winner in the Mexican league—tops each year in home runs, runs batted in, and batting average. A great hitter, Hector was so slow afoot you could whistle two choruses of "South of the Border" by the time he made it to first. But I worked with Hector, and I had him stealing bases. I taught him how to use what speed he had, how to anticipate moves, how to take an extra lead, how to get the jump on pitchers. Mostly, I worked with Hector on his bunting. By the end of the season Hector was an expert bunter.

We bunted, and we ran, and we stole bases. We played aggressive baseball. I was immensely pleased when every pitcher on the club became a good bunter, someone you could depend on. In batting practice, we had a rule—for every two good bunts a pitcher laid down, one to third and one to first, he was entitled to take two more full swings. They loved it. I made them earn the fun of swinging for the fences during practice. My ball club learned to bunt so well we were able to make twenty-two successful squeezes in a row, which should be a record in any league. The Mexicans, the fans and the players, called me *El Rey del Squeeze.* King of the squeeze.

They were a team in every sense of the word, and it

was a truly rewarding time in my life. After winning the championship game, we had a big team party, and the Carta Blanca flowed, and the players lifted me on their shoulders and they shouted, "Viva, Maury!" At that moment I felt warmer than the sauce we put on our tacos.

It was the first time, that winter in Hermosillo, that I was able to put my managing theories to the test. And I stole a pennant in Mexico.

Whether you are managing in Mexico or in the majors, the technique of discipline is always one of the tricky departments in the handling of players. Discipline, according to many interpretations of the book, is a simple matter of setting down one set of rules for all twenty-five players on the club. How often has it been said by a manager that no one player is bigger than the team (or in extreme cases of managerial rigidity in following the book: "No player is bigger than the game of baseball"). And that, I say, is about as fair and logical as paying all twenty-five players the same salary.

With twenty-five players on a squad, I would have twenty-five different sets of rules. If I had a Dick Allen—and I'd sure want a Dick Allen on my club—I would certainly not want him to follow the same rules as a fourth-string catcher.

The book method of handling ballplayers stipulates that in certain instances, if one player does violate a rule, the entire ball club should pay for it. This is reminiscent of the old military system in which the entire barracks is restricted for the weekend if one GI's shoes aren't shined. The theory is that the group pressure will force everybody to follow the rules.

Suppose a right fielder dogs it in a night game, and

as a result, the team loses. Your book manager will probably get a classic case of the red-ass and holler in the clubhouse, "All right, just for that it's morning workout for everybody tomorrow."

Today's young players cannot be treated in the old book tradition. They need more encouragement, more guidance, more explanation, more compliments—boy, do they ever need compliments! Actually, what today's young player would like life in baseball to be is one constant pat on the butt and a continuing flow of kind words. However, a compliment must always serve a purpose, and the manager must know his team so well that he knows when he should administer a kick instead of a pat on the butt.

Either it's a part of the book or it's old traditional baseball rigidity that after a defeat the clubhouse turns into a morgue—no talking, no jokes, all grim silence and solemnity. In Mexico I told my players that if they had given their best and still lost to a better team there was no need to hang our heads and act as though the sun would never shine again. In the wake of a defeat, I told them, we could still engage in normal conversation, we could tell our jokes, and if anyone had a harmonica, he could play it, win or lose.

Another dictum from long-standing tradition states that a player in a slump will invariably find himself turned into the dugout pariah. When he's on a hitting streak, he gets pounded on the back by the manager, the coaches, and his teammates, and everyone says, "Way to go, babe!"

Let him fall into a slump, as happens to all ballplayers, and on comes the silent treatment. I've seen it happen many times. Hell, it's happened to me, and when it did I wondered then if anyone gains when a player is suddenly treated as though he had contracted a contagious disease. A slump may be painful, but it isn't contagious. Yet if a player is taken out of the lineup for weak sticking, he can sit on the bench for weeks and the manager won't give him the time of day. When he's in a slump is exactly when a player needs help the most.

Not that I'd ever want to spoil a player, which is the same as spoiling a child. The Dodgers of my time, I believe, spoiled Willie Davis by pampering him at the start of his career, by not straightening him out on the fundamental errors he was committing, especially in attitude. The beginning is where the correcting must be done. And in that regard the key to managing is consistency. You don't let a kid put his hand in the cookie jar six days a week and then, on the seventh day, spank him for it.

As a manager I would have to convince the players that I have some knowledge of how they feel and think, that I was a player once myself and that I hadn't forgotten. My players would never find me playing the watchdog. For the benefit of the general manager, who is usually a man insistent on some form of protocol, I would impose a curfew, but for no other reason. At the clubhouse meeting I'd ask the players what they preferred.

"We've got to have a curfew. The club demands it. So what'll it be? You guys are the ones who'll have to keep the curfew, not me. So what do you want it to be?"

I suspect that they would settle for a curfew of three hours after the final out of a night game, which is usually ended at about ten thirty or close to eleven. On most clubs the general curfew rule in effect now is two and a half hours after the last out. Maybe a few of the players would vote for five hours after the final putout, but I would bet that they'd be voted down by the more sensible majority.

It's my feeling, based on my experience as a ball-player, that the players would want some kind of curfew imposed. Otherwise, where's the challenge? Once, in the minors, I was playing for Bobby Bragan, the fiery old catcher, and we were in Salt Lake City on a monstrously hot night. It was so hot that, as the team wit cracked, a dog was chasing a cat down the main street and they both were walking.

On this miserable, still Utah night, we were staying at a shabby hotel, without air conditioning. Bragan gathered us together.

"Look, you guys, no curfew tonight," Bragan announced. "Who can sleep in this heat? I'm not going to worry about some goddamn curfew on a night like this."

All the players let out a cheer. "See you later," Bragan said.

We played cards in the lobby, and then people started yawning and looking at their watches, and it was time to go upstairs. We recognized a basic fact of human nature—what's the fun in staying out if you aren't breaking any rules? And these were the same players who, on the night before, were squirming around trying to figure ways to get in and out of the hotel an hour before curfew. Later we came to the conclusion that wise old Bobby was cheating us out of our fun—and I was learning yet another lesson in the complex art of handling players.

On the subject of fines, I don't believe in the book theory that a club must take money from a player in order to make him perform better on the field. Here I disagree with the man I consider the smartest manager that baseball has ever seen. I refer to Leo Durocher.

Leo used to say, "Hit him in his bank account. It's the only place the son of a bitch feels it. I don't fine him for anything he can reach for." Leo would start his fines at $350, even more as inflation began to hit. Leo would strike at his players in the bank account instead of the wallet. He wanted the fined player to have to think about his transgression while he was waiting for payday, when his check would be lighter.

In general, I don't believe in fines coming from the ball club. If the players want to organize a little penny-ante system, I'm for it. I'm referring here to fines that will later add up to the funds for a team party. But I would hope they'd have so little in the kitty that they'd be forced to settle for beer instead of champagne.

A $5 fine for missing a sign is one example, but on the other hand, my signs would be so simple only a dummy could ever misread them. And that's another part of the baseball book—the complicated signs that force the third base coach to invent a new kind of funky chicken dance, the way he has to move around, fluttering and tapping at his cap and his uniform. There are managers who make the team signs so complex a batter needs an interpreter from the UN.

The players on my club might want to issue $5 fines for failing to deliver on a sacrifice bunt or for not running out an infield grounder aggressively. They could compile their own list of punishable offenses. But I contend that a manager should be able to convince his players of the importance of signs and other nuances of the game in other ways than through nibbling at a man's paycheck. Fines create resentment, not results.

How and when to fine a player is one of the many keys to the relationship of manager and players. I have seen managers who isolate themselves from their players, setting up a wall. Others try to become too close, and their emotions become involved in managerial decisions that should be dispassionate and objective. Neither of these extremes is effective. A manager must learn how to walk a delicate middle line. Most of all, he must convince the players to have full confidence in his fairness.

If one of my players is out after curfew and he sees me enter the bar, I wouldn't want him to spill his drink on his $200 outfit and run and hide. All I ask is that he give me—and the team—an extra 5 percent of effort in tomorrow's game.

There are few more distressing sights than a manager sitting in the hotel lobby after curfew, doing sentry duty, and I've seen them and made a mental note that I would never fall into that category. Often as not, a player sees him and goes into a panic, and then he loses an extra half hour of sleep trying to find another entrance to outsmart the manager. A manager should be a leader, not a watchful parent.

We learn from such observations, and I got an eyeful of how not to handle players in the first year I spent with the Pittsburgh Pirates under Harry "The Hat" Walker. The word around town that year went: "They got too many niggers on that team." Translated, what they really meant was: "They got too many niggers and they aren't winning." There is nothing like a winning team to make people color-blind, and we weren't winners. It applies not only to baseball, but to any sport. In pro basketball, where the blacks have come into dominance, there was a time when coaches were leery of putting too many blacks into the lineup—at least until Red Auerbach, in the middle of a game, had five blacks on the court for his Boston Celtics and the world didn't collapse. Before that happened, the saying about black basketball players went like this: "Play two at home, three on the road, and four if you're behind."

Anyway, we had thirteen black players on the Pittsburgh club, the largest number ever on a major-league roster. We also had the Latins, such as Roberto Clemente, Jose Pagan, Manny Mota, and a few others. I won't accuse manager Harry Walker of outright prejudice. But I will say that his attitude of at least obvious indifference to the needs of blacks and Latins was reflected on the overall playing of the club, and it set a tone of discontent. Discontent, hell! It was turmoil.

Harry Walker was the Gestapo in a hat. He was a nonsmoker and a nondrinker and a one-man police state. Harry the Hat wanted to govern his players twenty-four hours a day. Every night on the road he conducted his own bed check, often as late as four in the morning. Usually he would check the rooms twice in a night. A bed check by Harry the Hat would make a marine barracks inspection look like a social call at teatime.

Scene in a hotel: Harry Walker enters the elevator from the lobby. He sees two young women, each one carrying a drink in her hand.

"Would you like a drink?" one of the girls says to Harry.

"No, no, no," Harry says. "Say, where are you going?"

"Oh," she says, "we're seeing two baseball players from the Pittsburgh team. Maybe you know them."

Then she named the players, and (this the players learned later from the girls) Harry turned a few shades of crimson. They got off the elevator, and Harry did, too, walking in the opposite direction. After nearly a half hour, the Hat made his move.

He pounded on the door. "Lemme in! I know they're in there! Open this goddamn door!"

"Who is it?"

"It's me, the Hat. Goddammit, lemme in!"

The door was opened, and Harry burst in. He was face to face with two of his players. Without a word, he pulled back the drapes, and he looked in the closets. He pulled back the shower curtain. He ransacked the entire room.

"All right," Harry said. "I know they're here."

"Who's here, Hat?"

"There's no fire escape, there's no back door," Harry went on. "I don't know what in hell you did with those girls, but I'm going to get you for it. If it takes all season, I'll get you!"

Then he left, fuming and ranting down the hall.

Ballplayers under servitude to Harry "The Hat" Walker learn to be clever. I won't reveal any secrets, but there is a type of studio couch in this hotel that pulls back under a shelf. When the couch is pulled out, there is space under the shelf and if the girls are small enough. . . .

Once in Cincinnati, I was out playing my banjo at the Playboy Club and I came in a half hour after curfew. When I went back to the hotel, my roommate,

Willie Stargell, looked up from his bed and said, "Roomie, the man checked."

Then he told me what had happened. Harry the Hat had called on the phone, and Stargell answered. "Willie," the Hat said, "where's your roommate?"

"Uh, I think he's in the bathroom, Skip," Willie said.

"You know he's not in the bathroom," Walker said. "He's not there, right?"

"Yes, sir."

"Tell Wills when he comes in, it costs him three hundred dollars."

"Yes, sir."

"And it costs you a hundred for lying."

The next night Harry the Hat was on the phone again.

"Hell, he ain't here!" Stargell blurted, and hung up.

As it turned out, Walker fined me $700 for being a half hour late for curfew on two successive nights. But Willie wasn't going to get caught lying on that second night.

Story from Donn Clendenon: "I'm in my room, and the Hat knocks on the door. 'Open up. It's me. The Hat.' I tell him we're watching TV, me and Bob Veale. He says, 'Open up. I'm checking.' I opened the door and I tell Harry right to his face: 'If you take one move across the doorstep, I'll knock you right on your ass.' Harry couldn't talk he was so mad. He kind of sputtered and turned on his heel and walked out."

When the Pirates would check into the hotel in St. Louis, Harry "The Hat" Walker used to instruct the phone operator to connect the lines so that he could intercept any calls coming into the players' rooms. Every time a player would get a call the phone would ring in

Harry's room. He could hear everything, and the bells were always ringing.

There are few secrets on a ball club. The players soon learned about their manager's surveillance system. One night at the hotel several of the players gathered in one room and phoned a player in another room. They waited until it was obvious that the phone was being tapped by the Hat himself.

The conversation between the players' rooms went something like this:

"Did you see what a stupid move the Hat made tonight?"

"Yeah, we could've lost the game."

"How the hell did such a stupid son of a bitch ever make it to the big leagues?"

"Beats the hell outa me. He's the dumbest manager I ever played for."

A click on the phone. Harry the Hat had hung up. The players roared. It was one of the great nights of hilarity in Pirate history.

At nine thirty the next morning, the phones started ringing. Walker and his coaches were calling all the players to a ten o'clock meeting. For a ball club that had played a game the night before, ten in the morning is an awful hour. At ten Harry had all of us in the conference room, and he was so sore he could hardly speak.

But the words came popping out like machine-gun blasts: "I heard you! I heard you! I heard you!"

He looked from one player to the next, all around the room.

"I heard every word you said about me!" Harry yelled. "Dumbest manager, huh? I'm so dumb, huh,

I'm so dumb I was able to catch you stupid bastards talking about me. That's how dumb I am."

"Aw, Harry," one of the players said.

"Aw, Harry, my ass," Walker said. Then he looked right at me. "And you, Wills, I saw what time you came in here last night. You came in at three in the goddamn morning, and don't you try to deny it."

I couldn't deny it. The Hat had me dead to rights. I had been out playing my banjo at a Dixieland jazz club in St. Louis called Your Father's Mustache. But I had come in as stealthily as I could. I left my cab half a block from the hotel, I looked around carefully, walked in through the side entrance, and went up by the freight elevator. Nobody could have seen me.

"What do you mean, Hat?" I said, stalling.

"You know what I mean," Walker said. His face leered with triumph. "I'll tell you how I know. I was across the street in the park behind a tree. That's where I saw you from—behind a goddamn tree!"

It was unbelievable. There's a little park across the street from the hotel, and parks have trees, and this man, a manager in the big leagues, had been out there at three in the morning hiding behind a tree, trying to entrap his players.

Through the years, the smart managers in baseball have learned to follow a useful policy—it's called looking in the other direction. If a manager is watching every single move his players make over a period of seven long months, through spring training over 162 games and on road trips, there is no way out of it—he has to spot a player doing something he shouldn't do and right off there is trouble.

The book says that ballplayers have to be all-American boys, straight off the bubble-gum cards. Being human beings, they violate the rules, and they're in trouble, and if you have a manager who's watching all of the time, you will have players who are in trouble most of the time.

Personally, I have always liked Casey Stengel's rule. "I don't like my players drinking at the hotel bar," Casey once said, "because that's where I drink."

In my philosophy of handling players, instilling the proper mental approach ranks at the top. I have always believed that a team can't win without a positive mental approach, and nothing helps this along better than winning. Nobody on a ball club needs a pep talk during a winning streak. It's no secret that success breeds confidence. But to achieve success, first you must build a team's confidence, and that must come from the manager—and it comes first at spring training.

In all my years of observing the ritual of spring training, I have seen only the physical approach—how do you hold a fork ball, how do you pivot on a double play, how do you hold a bat? Rarely have I ever heard anybody in authority talk about the science of the game itself, how to win, the mental approach.

Talent provides an enormous edge—without talent a team isn't going to win. But a smart, alert mental approach can narrow the gap for the less talented. The pennant winners and the second division clubs are just as often separated by the mental approach, as well as the talent.

Aside from the superstars, the big-league ballplayers fall into two groups. The first type, constituting the big majority, are the big and talented athletes who are inclined to depend on their God-given skills. Then there are the players less gifted in size or natural ability, the scramblers who are compelled to use every ounce of their talent and every avenue of their brain—an Eddie Stanky comes to mind or a Gene Mauch or, yes, a Maury Wills.

This type of player knows that once he stops thinking of ways to outsmart the opposition, he's back in the bush leagues. He knows that the science of winning baseball is wrapped up in one word—surprise. You don't throw the book at the opposing club. You throw surprises, the unexpected.

In managing, I'd create this same mental approach, this same flair for guile and surprise, not only in the less talented but in all the players on my club. It can be done. You do it with leadership.

I wouldn't want any pipe smokers on my ball club— now that's obviously a figurative statement. Some of my best friends are pipe smokers. I smoked a pipe myself, briefly. I bought this beautiful pipe and filled it with aromatic tobacco. Feeling very debonair, I went into the clubhouse that night, puffing my new pipe. A moment later Pete Reiser, one of the Dodger coaches, came whipping at me and he grabbed that pipe out of my mouth and slammed it into the trash can.

"Why did you do that, Pete?" I said, dumbfounded. "That's my brand-new pipe."

"A pipe is a sign of a contented man," Reiser snapped. "I don't want you to be contented. No ballplayer should be contented."

I haven't had a pipe in my mouth since.

Pete Reiser happens to occupy a very special niche in my list of personal heroes. They used to call him Pistol Pete in the old Ebbets Field days, and he won the league batting title in 1941, and he probably set a record for running into walls in pursuit of line drives.

A dedicated player, Pete Reiser taught me dedication, which is a valuable attribute for anyone, player or manager. It was Pete who came to my rescue when I came up to the Dodgers and fell into a slump that might have sent me back to the minors. Hour after hour, for thirteen straight days, Pete coached me in batting, working alone in the oppressive heat of the Los Angeles Coliseum.

"This heat is too much. I can't take it," I'd say to Reiser.

"Would you rather take a little heat here with the Dodgers," said Pete, "or go back to the bus and wool-shirt circuit up in Spokane?"

Slowly and painfully, as Reiser pitched to me, I learned to become a major-league hitter. I owe my career in baseball to Pete Reiser, and I'll believe anything Pete tells me, even about pipe smokers.

Still, as I say, it's a figurative statement. Pipe smoking is merely a symbol for self-satisfied, nonhustling baseball. Pipe smokers never steal pennants.

In achieving a non-pipe-smoking, aggressive, positive mental approach in my players, I would want the assistance of a man who is better acquainted with the inner workings of the mind than anyone I have ever known. His name is Arthur Ellen, and he is a professional hypnotist.

Hypnotism is already starting to play a role in sports, but baseball is probably too tradition-bound to accept it very widely in my time. Nowhere in the baseball book is there any mention of hypnosis.

As the manager of a major-league team, one of my first moves would be to sign Arthur Ellen as a consultant. Arthur would come to spring training camp, he would have an office next to mine, and he would be available to the players from the first day. No player would ever feel compelled to seek out Arthur for help, but he would be there, and his door would always be open.

Arthur Ellen is an extraordinary man. He was teaching doctors and dentists how to use hypnosis when it was still a dirty word in medical circles. This was long before the American Medical Association voted to accept hypnosis as a useful healing instrument. In 1968 Ellen wrote a book called *The Intimate Casebook of a Hypnotist*. It is significant that a San Francisco physician, Dr. David B. Check, wrote a preface to the book, calling Ellen "a gifted student of psychology and a valuable colleague."

My first meeting with Arthur Ellen took place in Las Vegas, in the lounge of the Sahara Hotel. This was in the winter of '62 while we were working—Milton Berle and six of us Dodgers—in our act down the Strip at the Desert Inn.

Sandy Koufax was a part of the group, and he knew Ellen—he had once consulted him on breaking his cigarette habit. So Sandy brought me to see him, and it was one of the most fortunate meetings of my life.

In the background, as we sat in the darkened lounge, we could hear the Vegas sounds—the gamblers talking to the dice, the drone of the dealers, the clanging rhythms of the slot machines. It's a steady hum with its own lulling tension. It's the sound that always comes to mind when I think of Las Vegas.

Then I saw Arthur Ellen approach our booth. He's a man of medium size, graying at the temples, with a distinguished look about him. I looked for the piercing eyes I expected in a hypnotist. Ellen's eyes were no way unusual, but there was something special about them. I had seen that look before in the best of the doctors I've known. I've seen it in Dr. Robert Kerlan, the Dodgers' team physician, in his associate, Dr. Frank Jobe, in Bill Buhler, the Dodgers' trainer. It is the look of compassion.

So this was the man who had helped cure Jackie Jensen, a great all-around athlete, of his fear of flying. He had helped Sal Maglie, the pitcher, overcome the pain of his injured hip. I had heard of at least three singers who had seen Ellen before a performance— Harry Belafonte, Tony Martin, and Dennis Day. Each one had had voice trouble. A quick session with Ellen, and they were able to sing again. Later Ellen would help Bill Toomey, the 1972 Olympic decathlon champion, in his comeback.

Over the years Arthur Ellen has assisted such ballplayers as Orlando Cepeda, Roberto Clemente, and Frank Howard. When Frank went to see Ellen, he was deep in a slump and convinced that his baseball career had ended. That night he poled two home runs.

We talked briefly at the table. Then Ellen suggested that we go to his dressing room. Sandy remained at the booth.

When we were alone, Ellen began by telling me about hypnosis, what it could do and what it couldn't.

"Hypnotism," Ellen said, "can't cure a broken leg or a worn-out kidney. It won't cure any organic ailments, but it can help you live with yourself under such conditions."

He told me that hypnotism wouldn't create a talent that didn't exist before, that it cannot produce clairvoyance, that nobody can remain in an hypnotic trance by accident. He stressed the point that any suggestions with negative connotation to a subject's sense of personal morality would be disobeyed by anyone under hypnosis.

I had never heard hypnosis explained before in such detail. I sat and nodded. "Hypnosis, to put it another way, can't make you do anything you really wouldn't want to do," Ellen said. "You are not helpless; you're not under another person's will. This is very important for you to know this. Under hypnosis, you are in full control of your actions. Now, what I can do is get to your subconscious quickly and allow you to reveal your true feelings to me and, what's even more important, to yourself."

Then he smiled and said, "That's about it, champ."

Champ. It's one of Arthur Ellen's favorite words. Long afterward I realized that it is his way of instilling a positive frame of mind within yourself—you see yourself as a champion.

As I sat straight on a hard-backed chair, my confidence thoroughly won over, the hypnosis began. With only a few words—no abracadabra and no watch dangling like a pendulum—Ellen put me under, into my first hypnotic trance.

I released what turned out to be a torrent of words. I talked about my fears that my leg would have to be amputated because of the hemorrhages. I told him about the pressures that drove me. I told him about my experiences as the first black playing for Fort Worth in the Texas League in the 1950s. I told him how we black players always felt we were under the gun, patted on the back for doing well, rendering our services, and then it's back in the cage. I told him of deep personal issues that I had never revealed to anyone.

Afterward I felt as though I had come out of a sauna, cleansed, almost purified. I felt relieved of so many burdens that had weighed on me.

Perhaps I could have gained the same effect by talking to a competent psychiatrist, but for me Arthur Ellen was the best analyst there could be. Without Arthur's wise counsel, I think I could have ended up hating every white person on earth. With his insights into human behavior, he knew what was true about racial prejudice and what might be imagined or rationalized. He taught me that if we allow our frustrations and inhibitions to build, it doesn't take long before they overcome us. Ellen taught me that anxieties form mental blocks, and hypnosis can help you push them aside and function.

Five years later my confidence in Arthur Ellen was again fulfilled under unusual circumstances. It began with what is known in baseball as the message pitch. When it's thrown by a major-league pitcher, you get the message, all right, because it's aimed at your head.

It was early in the season, I was in a Pirates uniform, and we were playing the Giants in Pittsburgh. Ray Sadecki was pitching for San Francisco. His first pitch sailed over my head. Western Union couldn't have delivered a better message.

As a veteran I could assume a few privileges in my choice of equipment. One of these privileges involved the usual rule that says players must wear helmets at bat. Instead of a helmet, which is bulky, I chose to wear a fiberglass insert under my baseball cap. And that's why I would take less than kindly to a pitcher who threw anywhere near my head.

For Sadecki, that was message pitch No. 1. On his next throw he delivered the second message. This one was a fastball aimed at another vulnerable spot—my knees. Batting right-handed against a lefty, I spun around to avoid the ball speeding at me, but as I pulled my left leg to the side, my right knee was exposed. When the ball struck the knee, the pain coursed through my body. I stood in the batter's box, momentarily paralyzed. My God, it was painful!

This was the knee that had been hurt so badly. The cartilage was loose and floating around. But I could still function, the injury had almost healed, and I had proved that the doctors were wrong when they said I'd never be able to play ball again.

I could feel the knee swelling inside me until it felt as big as a baseball. The umpire waved me to first. I tried to run and settled for an awkward trot. I remained on the bag at first for two pitches before excusing myself from the game.

Later I was interviewed about the incident by Dick Stockton on KFKD-TV, in Pittsburgh. I said, "It appears to me that he was throwing right at me." Then I said, "I just hope he doesn't leave the league before I do, and I hope I don't leave the league before he does."

"Why is that?" Stockton asked.

"Because," I said, "I want to sting him."

I had my revenge pretty well planned. The easiest thing in the world would be to punch the ball toward first base so that it would have to be fielded by the first baseman and Sadecki would have to go over and cover the base on the throw. I guarantee that Sadecki would have gotten my message.

Several weeks later we were in San Francisco, and I took a stroll near the Giants' bench. I spotted Sadecki standing alone.

"Why the hell did you throw at me?" I said.

"Orders, Maury, orders," he said.

Sadecki went on to explain that he was acting on orders from Herman Franks, the Giants' manager.

"No law says you have to follow that kind of order," I said to Sadecki. "I'm still going to dump you on your ass, and don't you forget it."

Sadecki shrugged and walked away. I never did return the message to Ray Sadecki, but I was still bitter. The injury to my right knee was what took me from the Dodgers. It had changed my life. And here's a major-league pitcher taking an order that could ruin my career.

Within a month after that incident, my average had skidded from .350 to .240. In mid-stride, whether I was at bat or on the field, my right knee would lock at the damnedest times. And the pain got worse.

One night, about ten minutes before game time in Pittsburgh, I placed a long-distance phone call to Arthur Ellen in Los Angeles. I had been trying to reach him all day and I had become desperate. Finally, the operator was able to track him down.

Alone in the clubhouse—the players were all on the field by now—I talked on the phone with Arthur. Soon he placed me under hypnosis—and as I had always allowed myself to do in the past with him, I spilled out my problems.

Then he talked and I listened. The leg hurt terribly, yes, Arthur told me, but he wanted me to ask myself one question—was I using the injury and my dislike for the Pittsburgh manager, Harry "The Hat" Walker, as a convenient excuse? Think about it, Arthur said. We talked of more personal matters, all while I was under hypnosis, on the long-distance phone.

Vaguely, as though in a dream, I could hear the national anthem being sung in the background. With the last notes still echoing in the ball park, two of my teammates—Andre Rodgers and Jose Pagan—had come looking for me in the clubhouse. Arthur quickly snapped me out of the trance.

My eyes were still closed, the telephone in my hand. The ballplayers must have assumed that I had just heard tragic news. I could see the concern on their faces.

"No, no," I said, opening my eyes. "Everything is . . . all right."

When people ask me about hypnosis, I say that I can only vouch for what Arthur Ellen has done for me and for others I know about. I try to talk with Ellen once every month or two. If he detects a hard coat of negativism in my voice, he puts me into a hypnotic trance. Otherwise, we will talk as friends, and usually, as we talk, he'll find that I do have a problem that I want to discuss.

Today Arthur Ellen doesn't perform in supper clubs. He works mainly as a consultant out of his office in a medical-dental building in West Los Angeles.

Ellen believes implicitly that physical problems are often rooted in an emotional difficulty but one that always strikes in the most vulnerable area. A dancer complains of pains in his legs; a singer loses his voice; an actor can't remember his lines; an accountant gets headaches over his books.

What Ellen does then is to plumb into the subconscious through hypnosis. And usually the problem is all in the mind.

How would Arthur Ellen work with a baseball club?

I have my own ideas how I think this would come about. At first, the players would make jokes and stay away. Then one player, who was really troubled, would sneak in to see Arthur. When he was helped, he would pass the word along to the others. Soon Arthur would have my players knocking over those mental blocks, seeing life more positively and fulfilling their potential as professional athletes.

Still another aspect to the handling of players is the ability to teach. A manager must have all the qualities of a good teacher. Truly good teachers, from first grade on up to graduate school, are a rare and distinctive breed. I don't think teaching can be taught. The best teachers seem to be born with an innate quality of being able to pass on their enthusiasm and their knowledge. I wasn't given much in the way of physical size or natural athletic gifts, but somewhere in my bones there is a feeling for the subtle art of teaching. So many ballplayers lack the patience to teach others what may have come easily to them. Nothing came easily to me. But I do know how to teach what I know.

I've taught the fundamentals in the Arizona instructional league. With the Dodgers and also with the Pirates, I would give the lectures on baserunning and base stealing. I've conducted clinics for the armed services in Europe. Charley Finley, owner of the Oakland A's, hired me to teach Herb Washington, a track speedster, how to put his running ability into base stealing. And of course I've taught my specialty at the Dodgers' training camp.

There are managers moving from team to team in the majors with fewer qualifications. And there are players who do move into managing with no experience at all.

I am firm in the belief that I could produce a winning team in the major leagues. I'd like to put my knowledge of baseball and of handling players to use. The only way that can be done is to be in charge. I want to be in charge.

7

Trades, the Rising Sun, and the Missing Shortstop

FOR a manager, trading is a roll of the dice. Trading is the tricky waters of baseball, full of unpredictable currents. Trading is also the most difficult way to steal a pennant. It's possible for a ball club to win one pennant with a flurry of trades for key players, but rarely, on the basis of a trade of two, can you win more than once. Generally, the best route to victory is by bringing up players through the farm system.

Trading is hoping. General managers—and they are, of course, the ones who authorize deals—trade for what they hope will happen. There's never been a general manager who is so brilliant that he can ever guarantee a sure-shot trade. Show me a general manager with a reputation as a shrewd trader, and I'll show you a man who's been lucky.

There are also times when trading is a matter of sound judgment, as well as luck. In 1974 the Dodgers traded pitcher Claude Osteen to the Astros to get Jimmy Wynn. For the Dodgers it was a steal because Wynn helped bring them a pennant whereas Osteen had one of his lesser seasons. Was it merely luck, a case of betting on the right horse? Not this time. The Dodgers have to be given credit for knowing that Jimmy Wynn was not, as the Astros must have believed, over the hill.

In theory, as a general rule, I would not want to trade away a slugger for a pitcher. Since pitchers are considered the most valuable merchandise in baseball, usually you have to give up too much to get a good one. The odds are against you. Besides, as the most fragile of athletes, so many things can go wrong with a pitcher. A pitcher can be a Secretariat one year and then turn overnight into a candidate for the glue factory.

It's also a pretty good rule of thumb to trade for specific needs and not for the variety of other reasons that players are acquired. For instance, if I had three Roberto Clementes, I wouldn't trade for a fourth Roberto Clemente. The best policy is to trade for immediate help. The Texas Rangers, to cite an example, were helped immediately when they engineered the deal with the Cubs to get Ferguson Jenkins. The Cardinals were helped immediately when they acquired Lou Brock for Ernie Broglio, who never did get out of the starting gate.

Unless you can receive exactly what you need to win a pennant, it's a self-defeating policy ever to trade a good player to another contender. The good players, if they must be traded, should go to a last-place club that doesn't figure to hurt you. And it's still better if you don't have to trade a good player until you sense that he's just about ready to lose a step. "Never wait until he breaks both legs" is the old baseball saying. In other words, trade a player while he's still marketable, and then it isn't such a risky roll of the dice.

It seems to me that when players are traded, too many things go unsaid. The personal touch too often is missing. Being traded, a player must adjust to new surroundings, and a manager is the one to make him feel welcome. I've seen players traded to a new club, and they are greeted by the manager with a handshake and a smile and then forgotten.

A manager must go beyond the amenities. It's his job to help the player produce on the field by making him a part of the team immediately. I would sit with a new player and talk with him, perhaps help him if he needed an apartment or a house for his family. There is no such thing as a player relations man on any club but it's the manager's responsibility to fill that niche. Why must a new player wait for the others to approach him, or why must he introduce himself to his new teammates? It's the manager's function to introduce a new player to every other player on the team, one by one. A small matter, perhaps, but it can be a necessary and helpful one in terms of the overall team feeling. In all my years in baseball I have yet to see a manager perform this simple act of courtesy.

I have always felt that a newly arrived player should never be rushed into the lineup even if he's traveled only an hour or two. So many times I've noticed that players get off an airliner after flying most of the day, and at night the manager puts them into a game. I wouldn't even have him pinch-hit for me until he's had time to soak up the atmosphere of his new ball club.

Too many things also go unsaid in regard to the other players on the squad. I have never yet seen a manager who would explain to the other players why a trade was made. When a player joins a new club after a trade, he has to be accepted by his teammates. That may be a slow process. A player might be resented by his new teammates who could have lost a buddy in the trade. As an example of this, I would cite Chris Chambliss, who came to the Yankees in a trade and ran into a difficult period of being accepted, which obviously affected his play. In such cases, a manager would be wise to ease the way.

Trading should be the result of a mutual agreement between the manager and the general manager. As a manager I would insist that no trades be instigated by the front office without my knowledge or even my consent. I have seen managers rendered helpless in this type of situation, their authority diluted. I would never want to be a puppet manager, and I've seen them, too.

When a star player is traded without the manager's knowing about every detail, it can result only in an uneasy situation. I don't believe, for example, that Walter Alston was personally involved in the trades that brought Dick Allen and Frank Robinson—and Maury Wills, too—to the Dodgers. It is one reason for Alston's longevity as a manager. He never bucks the front office in regard to trades.

There are any number of reasons for trades, and marquee power, which is almost as important in baseball as it is in show business, is one of them. A prime example would be Willie McCovey, the veteran first baseman who was obtained by the San Diego Padres in a trade with San Francisco before the start of the 1974 season. It wasn't likely that McCovey could blast out those thirty home runs a year as he had in the past, but he proved that he could still bring people into the ball park. His name sold tickets, and his presence created excitement.

Buzzie Bavasi, president of the Padres, engineered that trade for McCovey, and it was Bavasi, when he was general manager of the Dodgers, who put into practice one of the smartest moves a club can make.

Whenever a player was traded to the Dodgers, no matter how he may have played in the previous season, Bavasi would raise his pay.

This is very rare and very wise. A player traded to the Dodgers has to feel good about it, anyway, coming to Los Angeles and joining a club that's almost always in contention—and now he gets a raise in pay to boot. Now you have a player who's really going to bust his butt for Buzzie.

As a manager I would want a newly traded player to realize that it is the best of all possible worlds if he enjoys immediate success. Then he not only helps himself and the team, but also pleases the general manager, who can take his bows as a genius. It's customary for a general manager to give the player he has traded for every opportunity to make good. There'll never be a better time for a player to prove his worth—or for a manager to inspire him to play his best. A manager might do worse than inherit a team consisting of newly traded players, all of them eager to show the world that the club that traded them made a mistake.

The only flaw there—and every seemingly ideal situation will have a flaw—is that for the traded player his period of adjustment can go either way, and therein lies the gamble for the manager. When I was picked up on the expansion draft by the Montreal Expos, I played poorly. I was the same player when I was traded back to the Dodgers, where I felt at home, and two years later I was the major-league shortstop of the year. Few managers could have predicted that turn of events.

As everyone should know by now, there's not much sentiment in baseball. The old players move on, the young ones take their place, and the game continues.

Players must be traded or released. It's a part of the game. But if I were managing a big-league club, I know I'd have more concern for players than I've witnessed throughout my career.

I think back to the time in Pittsburgh when I saw Bill Henry in the clubhouse, cheerfully putting on his uniform. He ran out onto the field, and in five minutes he had returned, his head down, his face drained of emotion.

The clubhouse attendant had just told him that he had been released by the Pirates. Bill Henry had been a major-league ballplayer for fourteen years, and he had to learn about his release from a clubhouse attendant.

All too often a player learns of his trade or release from the news media. He hears it on the radio as he's driving home from the ball park. Or he's called at home by a reporter who assumes that the player knows. Or he reads about it in the morning paper.

It is best, I think, for a manager not to become too close to a player's family. A manager who's thinking always of the good of the club can't permit himself to be swayed by personal relationships. But at least he can tell the player face to face in the privacy of his office. For me, it would be an unvarying rule, a principle of human relations.

This is merely part of what I feel should be the manager's responsibility toward his players. If a player must be released after long service to a club—or if he's a ten-year man and prefers retirement to a trade—then the manager should have some concern for his future. Usually, the general managers and owners of big-league clubs are well situated in a community. They know their way around the workings of the power structure. A phone call by an owner to a friend could give the old player a shot at a new profession. Often that's all that it takes, a phone call and some consideration. Possibly there are examples of this happening. But I don't know of any.

In recent years the major leagues have installed a rule about trading that makes sense. It states that a player who has served ten years in the majors has the right to veto a trade. Ron Santo, for one, turned down the trade that would have sent him from the Cubs to the California Angels. The average length of a player's stay in the majors is said to be four years, but there are still a number of ten-year men who now have some kind of choice that they didn't have before.

The ten-year rule may be one step toward a loosening of the reserve clause, which baseball likes to call the glue that holds the structure of the game together. The reserve clause means simply that a player is bound to one club until he is traded, is released, is put on waivers, or retires.

Without the reserve clause in effect, baseball executives say the fabric of the entire game would be unraveled. They contend that if a ballplayer could choose wherever he wanted to play, every player would head for the richest owner and the promise of the most money. The result, they tell us, would be chaos.

From a manager's point of view, it might be dismaying to think of players suddenly taking off in hopes of a fatter contract elsewhere. And possibly it would happen that way, but I doubt it. I don't think it would happen because the owners of major-league clubs are too smart to permit it. The owners know that all the links in the chain have to be at least fairly strong. Weak clubs hurt the game and downgrade the level of competition, and obviously, this would be reflected in the gate receipts.

If the reserve clause were discarded, I wouldn't foresee any wholesale jumping of players from club to club. What would happen more likely is that the owners who are tight with a dollar would have to come up to the others in what they pay their ballplayers.

The owners, being friends as well as competitors, would never allow one or two clubs to grab off all the players and develop into perennial powerhouses. They would sit down and work out a system of their own, and that system would involve paying ballplayers more money all down the line.

Managers, as they grow older, tend to have convenient lapses of memory. They tend to forget their own feelings when they were playing; they will often become callous and remember only dimly how it felt to be traded. Being traded is one of the facts of baseball life. A player lives with the likelihood that at some point in his career he will be uprooted by a trade, and it is accepted—although never completely—as inevitable.

Some players still feel a sense of humiliation when they are traded, and a manager is derelict if he doesn't respond to the need in such cases for reassurance. The player might feel that his old club had no further use for his talent and now he's being disposed of like an old piece of Kleenex. A trade to him is a sign of incompetence, that he can't do the job.

But that isn't always true. A trade isn't necessarily a put-down. Different clubs have different needs. A team must give up one or more players to bring in the player who's needed. When the Dodgers traded Willie Davis for Mike Marshall in 1974, neither player should have felt slighted. The Dodgers needed a strong relief pitcher, the Expos needed a strong center fielder, and the deal was made.

A manager of a New York club will never find himself greeting a newly traded player who feels abused. Playing in New York puts a ballplayer in the nation's communications center, and there's always more press and publicity. Players also rarely complain if they're sent to the Cubs because they know they'll be playing only day baseball in Wrigley Field.

The manager of a contender won't have a grumbling player on his hands, either, when he comes to the club in a trade. And players like to be traded to a club that uses a lot of chartered flights instead of commercial flights, which mean hours of hanging around airports. Players also like the idea of being traded to the Dodgers, a club that has its own team plane. Besides, playing in Los Angeles puts a ballplayer on the television and movie scene. It's tough for a ballplayer in Cincinnati to get tapped for a TV commercial or an acting role—unless you're Johnny Bench. But if Johnny were playing in Los Angeles, he would be as familiar a figure on TV as the late Euell Gibbons munching hickory nuts.

Managers must realize that for a ballplayer, being traded anywhere is usually an inconvenience, and sometimes it's a hardship. I've seen players come to a city in a trade, and before they're even established, they begin to put down roots. They buy a home in the mistaken belief they're set for a lifetime—and then they're traded. It might be a jinx, buying a new home. As soon as Ted Sizemore bought a new home in Los

Angeles, before the ink was ink dry on the escrow papers, the Dodgers had traded him to St. Louis for Dick Allen.

Time was, another sure way to be traded was to be named the player representative by one's teammates. Usually the player rep was picked because he was the sharpest guy on the club, the best with figures, and just as often he was a second-string utility player and therefore highly vulnerable to be traded. Soon the player rep became the designated target for trading.

Within the last six or seven years the players looked around and saw what was happening to their elected representatives. Was it merely a coincidence that they didn't seem to last very long? It was about then that the name players, the stars on the club, were talked into taking a stand as player reps. It was clearly a smart move. What manager is going to allow his club to trade a star just because he's a player rep? Dave Giusti with the Pirates, Don Sutton on the Dodgers—both are player reps and not likely to be dealt away.

Actually, the player rep doesn't have all that much power. It's his job to lay out the facts before the players, and they are the ones who reach the decisions. But it's the player reps who relay the players' decisions to management, and everybody knows about the emperor who would be given bad news from the messenger and then order his head lopped off.

When Marvin Miller came in to organize the players' association, the player representative became more than a figurehead. I believe Miller was good for baseball in at least one respect—he fought for a boost in the minimum salaries a club could pay a ballplayer, and any manager who forgets that a player does better with an equitable paycheck is kidding himself.

At the time Miller arrived on the scene, the minimum salary for a major-league ballplayer was $7,500, and there were quite a few players making only that minimum or not much above it. For a single player, that was meager enough, but a player with a family could hardly make it. Usually, he has to maintain two homes, he has to dress like a big leaguer. He doesn't have to drive a Lincoln Continental, but even a Pinto costs.

In time, the minimum gradually went up to $15,000. But there's a fallacy here because the fans read about the Dick Allens and the Hank Aarons and the others who make their $200,000 or $100,000, and they see the ballplayer as spoiled and overpaid. They don't realize that it's the $100,000-plus player who helps bring the average big-league salary up to what it is—$38,000 a year.

Now I am totally against reading another man's pocket. I don't believe in saying what another man should be able to afford. I'm referring here to the owners of the ball clubs, the men who take the risks and deserve whatever they make. But I am opposed to the way that athletes are made to look greedy when they try to get a bigger piece of the pie.

Salaries of the players aren't that big an item in the operation of a ball club. The total salaries add up to something like 17 percent of the money involved in baseball. With concession sales, season ticket sales, parking fees, and, most of all, broadcasting rights, many clubs have their players' salaries paid back into the till even before opening day.

Consider Hank Aaron, whose contract at Atlanta called for more than $200,000 a year. On the first few road swings in '74 the Braves had visited three or four cities, had filled the park wherever they went at $4 or more a head—and Aaron's salary was paid.

Nobody can tell me that Hank Aaron was ever overpaid. In professional sports an athlete who makes big money has earned it by bringing big money into the club. More money for ballplayers helps everybody, including the manager.

Of all the reasons for trading a player, the least acceptable is spite and anger coupled with misunderstanding. It happened that way to me when I was the missing shortstop in the Land of the Rising Sun. This particular episode may never occupy more than a footnote to baseball history, but since so many accounts have been written about the time I left the Dodgers on a tour of Japan, I want to tell my side of the story for the first time.

Actually, the incident in Japan had its beginnings nearly six months earlier on a July night in Shea Stadium in 1966. Jack Fisher was pitching for the Mets, Don Drysdale for the Dodgers. With two out and nobody on base, Fisher, a good hitter, cracked a double to left-center, and now he was perched at second base. Our next move was to pick him off.

Base stealing is my business, and I could often tell when a runner had eyes for taking the base. The tipoff is the reaction of the runner after he gets his signal from the coach. If the runner is at first and he gets the sign to go, he will almost always turn his head and look at second base as though the bag were going to move if he didn't. A runner with no larceny in his soul will never look at the next base.

Drysdale was one of the best actors in baseball. When they talk about pickoff moves that nobody could detect, Drysdale should have been up for an Oscar. Now Fisher was extending his lead. I flashed a signal to John Roseboro, behind the plate, and he flashed it back to Drysdale—and he whirled and threw straight at second base. I charged at Fisher with the ball in my hand. But he had already taken off for third and I assumed we had him nailed.

Fisher is a big, heavyset man and I knew I could track him down on the base path. Old baseball rule: Never throw the ball unless it's necessary. I had some speed in my favor, and Fisher was supposed to be slow. He turned to be a big, heavyset guy who could run.

I was chasing after him, holding the ball in my right hand—and he was going like the wind. Fisher was like an elephant, picking up speed with each step. I made a quick mental note: Never let an elephant get the jump on you.

I kept after him, ball in hand, until I was about six feet from third base and I still hadn't caught him. I had one chance—I dove headfirst, with my right arm extended for the tag. I hit him on the bottom part of his legs, and he tripped and then he rolled over on top of me, his weight landing directly on my right knee. The pain stung like fire.

There's another old baseball saying: He won't rub, which means that when a player is hit by a pitched ball or hurt otherwise, he won't yield to his pain by rubbing where it hurts. He will wait until he gets back to his dugout, and then he can rub and holler. I did something like that.

Certainly I didn't want to let Jack Fisher, a pitcher, know that my knee was injured. Pitchers have a way of accidentally throwing in the direction of injured parts of the body.

In the next half of the inning I went to bat and laid down a good bunt along the third base line. Halfway down to first, I felt a terrible pain—it was my knee. I was helped off the field.

The Mets' team physician examined my leg. "You've had it, Maury," he said. "The cartilage has popped. You'll have to have surgery on this leg. You're out for the year."

That was impossible. I had played before with a broken toe after Jimmy Edwards of the Reds had come on like a ton of bricks at second base and kicked my right foot. Only our general manager, Buzzie Bavasi, and our team physician, Dr. Robert Kerlan, knew about that broken toe. I had played with a leg that was hemorrhaging internally. I had often played hurt. I knew something about pain.

We were in first place in a tight pennant race. I wasn't about to get out of the lineup. The next day our trainer, Bill Buhler, wrapped the knee tightly with tape, with the cartilage rolling around inside. With the putting on and taking off of the tape, I finally was left with no skin, only bare flesh, from my calf to about eight inches above the knee. Anyway, we won the pennant and lost the World Series. But I played all the way.

After the World Series the Dodgers were invited on a playing tour of Japan by the Japanese government. It was, we were given to understand, entirely voluntary. Several of the Dodgers said they couldn't go or didn't want to go, and they were excused, Sandy Koufax, Don Drysdale, and Wes Parker among them. With my injured knee, I expected to be included among the no-shows. But Walter O'Malley wanted me to go.

Buzzie Bavasi said to me, "You're the captain of the team. They want to see you over there. If you can't play, just go along there, be there, sign autographs. But Mr. O'Malley wants you there——so go!"

The Dodgers left for Japan, and I went to Las Vegas. Now it was in the papers that the Japanese are raising hell because the Dodgers were coming without their little shortstop. The Japanese people would naturally relate to a fellow of my size.

The Dodgers tracked me down in Vegas. "All right, we made an agreement," I said. "I'll go, but I can't play."

In Tokyo we were playing the Tokyo Giants and winning by about 16–1. Preston Gomez, coaching at third, trotted into the dugout. "You two guys," Preston said, pointing to Ron Fairly and Tommy Davis, "don't have to finish the game."

That's when I volunteered to play. It was foolish, but I was swept up in the moment, hearing the Japanese fans cheering. Maybe I wanted them to do some cheering for me. I waited out a base on balls and reached first. Now the Japanese fans picked up the chant: "Go, go, go!"

If I could have made an announcement over the public address system that my leg was hurt and I couldn't steal, so please forgive me, folks, I would have done that. Instead, I realized I had better at least try for a steal.

I slid into second base on that knee and the pain jolted me into the ground. Don't rub, and I didn't. But at the end of the inning I took myself out of the game.

The next day we were losing, 8–0, to a local hero, a pitcher they called the Japanese Larry Jaster after the Cardinals' left-hander who had beaten us five straight games that year. I reminded Preston Gomez to tell Walt Alston that I wasn't supposed to play.

A few minutes later, Alston walked into the dugout

and said to everybody in general, "Goddammit, if you guys didn't want to play, you shouldn't have come over here."

I played.

The next day we were in northern Japan, in Sapporo, the site of the 1972 Winter Olympics, and the rain was pouring throughout the morning. At game time it was still drizzling. But the game was on, and I was in the starting lineup.

I hit a double, and as I stood at second base, I knew there was no way I was going to try to steal third, not in that mud and not on my injured knee. Somebody hit a single and soon I was rounding third. With my left foot I touched the inside of the bag, and at once the leg crumbled under me.

Pain coursed through my body. I was down on one knee, and Gomez was leaning over me.

"My God, Preston," I said. I closed my eyes, and the pain contorted my face. As I say, pain is no stranger to me, but this time the ache seemed deeper and more penetrating.

I lifted myself up slowly. Then I glanced at the Dodger bench. Walt Alston turned his head away.

I said to myself, "Friend, the only way you're going to play baseball next year is to go home and get off this knee."

Without asking approval, I took myself out of the game. Walt Alston still wouldn't look at me as I sat, motionless, on the bench.

Two hours later we were on the team plane, heading back to Tokyo. There I phoned Walter O'Malley.

"Mr. O'Malley, this is Maury Wills," I said. "I know you're busy, but I'd like to see you for just one minute."

"What is it you want to see me about?" he said.

"I'd rather talk to you in person, Mr. O'Malley."

He made it clear that whatever I had to tell him could be spoken now on the telephone.

"I want to see you, Mr. O'Malley, about going home. My leg is hurt. I can't play. I want to go home."

There was a brief silence. "You can't do that," Mr. O'Malley said. "We are here as baseball ambassadors. How would it look to our hosts, the Japanese people, if you went home? No, Maury, you cannot go."

"Is that your final word, Mr. O'Malley?"

"My final word."

The phone clicked. I held the phone in my hand and stared at it. My leg was still throbbing with pain. I went downstairs to the lobby, picked up my passport, and then I went to the airlines counter and bought a ticket to Honolulu. There were Dodger players and Japanese officials in the lobby. I spoke quietly and tried to affect an air of calm.

What followed could have been lifted out of a spy thriller. A friend of mine in Japan, an importer from Los Angeles named Dave Warsaw, had left a car and a Japanese driver at my disposal.

"You're coming up with me," I told the driver and led him to my room. Pee Wee Oliver, one of the Dodger players, and I were roommates on the tour. Early the next morning, while Pee Wee was in the shower, the driver carried my bags downstairs and put them in the car. Minutes later I was on the elevator. On the next floor, I was joined by Red Patterson, the Dodgers' vice-president in charge of public relations and promotion.

"Up bright and early, Maury?" he said.

"Uh, yes, Red," I said.

"I thought I'd have a quick breakfast before we fly to Osaka," Red said. "Won't you join me?"

"Uh, no, Red," I said. "Got a couple things to do."

I remained on the elevator to the garage below. I found my car and driver, and we went to the airport. I went to the airline counter and checked my bags to Honolulu. Several feet away I noticed a Japanese newspaper writer and a photographer.

"Maury Wills," the photographer said, raising his camera and smiling.

"Please, no pictures," I said. I must have sounded like a movie star at a Hollywood premiere. "It's very important," I said. "No pictures, please."

The photographer nodded, a puzzled look on his face. But he put down his camera.

I went into the airport restaurant and lodged myself in a corner. As I looked out the window, less than 400 feet away, I could see the Dodgers' charter plane and some of the players coming down the ramp from another area in the terminal. When I saw several Dodger officials talking with a man from the airlines, I had to assume they were talking about the missing shortstop.

Not long afterward the plane taxied out to the runway and was soon bound for Osaka. My driver came to me. "They are good friends," he said, indicating the Japanese writer and photographer, who still lurked nearby. "Can they take pictures now?"

"All right," I said, "when I'm getting on the plane."

The next day the picture appeared in the paper along with a story that I had left the team and was going back to the States. My original plan had been to go to Honolulu for one day—I had never been there before—and then go on to Los Angeles. But when I got there, I learned that Honolulu is an exceptionally pleasant place to visit.

One night I went to a nightclub where the featured performer was a singer named Don Ho. I had never heard of him before. Don Ho was so good I was back the next night. Someone recognized me in the audience and told Don Ho who asked me to come up and sing. I don't have to be asked twice. I was on the bandstand singing with Don Ho for the next three nights. I didn't learn until years later that while I was singing one night in walked Buzzie Bavasi and his wife, Evit, who had flown over from the mainland. Buzzie told me that he walked in that night, took one look at his singing shortstop, and quickly walked out.

One day in Honolulu I spotted the headline in one of the newspapers—MAURY, WHERE ARE YOU? The story related that I had jumped the team in Japan and reporters and photographers were keeping a watch for me at the Los Angeles and San Francisco airports. Well, I wasn't ready to walk into that just yet.

One night, at the Hawaiian Village, I was listening to the Dixieland music. Again I was recognized, and the banjo player offered me his instrument, and again I didn't have to be asked twice. There were Los Angeles people in the audience, including Clint Eastwood, the actor, and a woman I didn't know—she was the one who left the next day and, when she arrived in Los Angeles, phoned the papers.

"You want to know where Maury Wills is?" she said. "He's in Honolulu, playing the banjo in a Dixieland club."

And so the story was printed that I had jumped the ball club to play banjo in a Dixieland club. A few nights later I went to the Honolulu auditorium where Sammy Davis, Jr., was appearing in concert. After the show, I was in his dressing room, with Sammy Davis and Peter Lawford.

As we talked, a big man bolted into the dressing room and whipped out a pad and pen. "Mr. Wills," he said, "I'm a reporter for a Honolulu paper."

I stood up. "I'd rather not talk now," I said.

But he Bogarted me. He moved right in so that I couldn't budge. At that moment Sammy Davis' bodyguard, who had some size himself, stepped between us.

"Problem?" the bodyguard said. He was as big as a door.

"No problem," I said. "Everything's fine."

The bodyguard grabbed the reporter with one hand behind his collar and the other hand with his belt in the back and lifted him out of the dressing room.

The next day the paper had a big story about how I had ordered Sammy Davis' bodyguard to abuse a reporter.

It was time for me to leave Honolulu. Altogether I stayed there eleven days. In Los Angeles I phoned Buzzie Bavasi. "Dammit, Buzzie," I told him, "you know I wasn't supposed to play at all over there."

Buzzie was sympathetic. "Mr. O'Malley is pretty hot about the whole thing," he said. "Maybe he'll cool off. I'll try my best to smooth it over. But you really did jump the ball club. You asked for trouble."

Now the reports circulated that Mr. O'Malley was furious and that he had to apologize for my actions to the premier of Japan and that, as a result, I had been placed on the trading block. The story was that Mr. O'Malley had told Bavasi: "Get rid of Wills."

By now I was in the gym working out, trying to get

my leg in condition for the next season. A story went out on the wire service that I was anxious to make amends to be at my best next year for the Dodgers.

Then Sandy Koufax announced his retirement. A hopeful thought crossed my mind: *With Sandy retiring, would the Dodgers want to trade me?* I nursed the hope that the club wouldn't want to lose two name players.

I reasoned that I had acted on my own convictions to leave Japan. It was my first conflict with the ball club. I thought of all the times I had played with injuries and the dedication I felt as a Dodger. And yet—Mr. O'Malley is the owner, he pays the bills. It's his ball club, and the trip to Japan was extremely important to him.

Bavasi told me that Mr. O'Malley was still on an around-the-world trip but that we would get together, the three of us, when he returned. "I'll do my best," Buzzie said.

A week passed. Mr. O'Malley still hadn't returned. I told Buzzie that I had to go home to Spokane. Buzzie, I realized, could only be an intermediary. If Mr. O'Malley couldn't be persuaded, then the burden of my actions would have to fall on me.

On December 1, Tom Harmon, the former football star who had become a Los Angeles sportscaster, phoned me in Spokane. He had his tape rolling for the interview.

"The winter baseball meetings have just started," Tom said in his crisp voice. "The rumor is that you've been traded to the Pirates. How do you feel about it?"

"I don't want to be traded, Tom," I blurted out. "I've spent all my life playing for the Dodgers. The Dodgers *are* my life. Tell the people of Los Angeles that I'm praying I won't be traded. Tell them I had to leave the team in Japan to rest my leg and save my career."

Half an hour later Harmon called me back.

"Maury, the interview we just did, it's past tense," he said. "It's on the wire now—you've been traded to Pittsburgh."

At that moment I felt as though I'd been slugged in the pit of my stomach. Seconds passed before I could speak. Whatever I said afterward I said quickly. I remember that I chose my words carefully, speaking of the Dodgers and of Mr. O'Malley without malice.

I had often read about ballplayers being traded and then they knock their former employers. It was a part of the book. When a trade is thought of as rejection, the first reaction usually is anger. I had vowed that if I were traded, however I felt privately, there would be no anger in my public statements. But I did feel very empty.

As a result of Mr. O'Malley's insistence that I be traded, the Dodgers went against the baseball rule and dealt me to another contending National League club. Bavasi also looked into the possibility of trading me to the Yankees, who had expressed some interest. But the Pittsburgh offer was apparently the best.

In analyzing the intent of trades, it's interesting to study this particular trade from the Pirates' standpoint. Should a ball club attempt to trade for a player who's been hurting them? If you can't beat 'em, should you get 'em to join you? It could be a sound maneuver for any trader to consider. The Pirates knew me well. There was a magazine story at the time that detailed how well.

The story pointed out that I had stolen more bases against the Pirates than any other team in the league and that I had built up a lifetime average of .350 against Pittsburgh pitching. In one game against the Pirates the previous year, I had singled, stole second and third, and trotted home with the winning run.

The next night, the story noted, I had bunted for a single, moved to second on an error by the pitcher, forced a balk by the pitcher and advanced to third, and then scored. Later I had driven in a run with a triple to give the Dodgers a 3–1 victory. Two days after that, in the twelfth inning, I hit a single to beat the Pirates, 5–4.

Altogether that added up to three games I had helped win for the Dodgers over the Pirates. And it was by a margin of three games that the Pirates had lost the pennant. For the Pirates, it was obviously a smart trade.

When I went to the Expos in the expansion draft, two years later, for me it was another taste of rejection. There are few cities in the Northern Hemisphere more cosmopolitan than Montreal. I liked the city, but what I liked most about Montreal was playing for Gene Mauch, a superlative manager.

What I liked least was playing in Jarry Park in the spring, if spring is the word for the first half of the season in Canada. Mark Twain once said that the coldest winter he ever spent was an August in San Francisco. I don't think old Mark ever played ball in Montreal.

Just before opening day, the field was resod—they couldn't do any resodding earlier because the ground was frozen. The infield was frosted, hard in some spots, as soft as French pastry in others.

We were playing the Cardinals on opening day in the freezer. The first grounder hit to me skittered through my legs. The fans started to boo. I don't think they ever stopped booing me in Jarry Park.

It would not be an exaggeration to say I was booed out of the country. At least the French-Canadians of Montreal were polite about their booing. Instead of booing me in French, a language I don't understand, the Montreal fans booed in English. They made that gesture so that I could understand every word of their pointed criticism.

The longest I have ever been booed at one time in my career was fifteen minutes, by the good fans in Montreal. Shouldn't that be in the books as a record for booing an infielder on foreign soil? What's so strange about this is that their disapproval came after I had pulled off one of my favorite plays and one, I might add, that as a manager I would want my infielders to know.

We were playing the San Diego Padres. Nate Colbert was on first, and at that time Nate could really fly. It was a one-out situation, and Al "The Bull" Ferrara was at bat. The Bull was a slow runner. He hit a pop fly just out of the infield. Colbert stayed close to first, expecting an easy catch.

Instead, I let the ball drop to the ground in front of me. Then I picked up the ball and threw it to second base. This forced out the fast runner, Colbert, and put the slow runner, Ferrara, on first. As a play, it is indisputably sound.

To the fans, however, I was the ballplayer who couldn't catch an easy fly ball. They started booing and hollering. I learned later that the broadcasters were criticizing my ineptness on the air. I said to myself: "Hell, at least Gene Mauch knows, at least my teammates know what I did."

A full inning later, the word must have buzzed around the ball park. They flashed an explanation in English and French on the scoreboard. "Maury Wills

should be applauded for an outstanding play," the
message said, or words to that effect. Then they explained the strategy of the play in detail. Now the fans
applauded. Justice had triumphed in *La Belle Pro-
vince.*

Later in the season the Dodgers came to town. I
wanted desperately to play well against my old team.
The first ball hit to me slashed through my legs. The
second grounder bounced off my left leg. We played
three games against the Dodgers, and I made those errors and went hitless. I was miserable. After the last
game I was sitting alone in the Montreal dugout. Don
Sutton, who had pitched for the Dodgers, came by and
shook hands.

"Captain," Sutton said, "you're still our captain.
Hang in there."

I was grateful for those words. I thanked Sutton and
walked into a rest room next to the dugout, and I
locked myself in. There, in the darkness, I beat my fists
against the wall.

It wasn't long after that day that we were in San Diego to play the Padres. We were staying at the LeBaron
Hotel, not far from San Diego Stadium, and I was
standing next to the hotel swimming pool, flipping
coins into the water. Kids were scurrying around the
pool, diving into the water to retrieve the coins in the
warm sun.

I heard someone call my name from a nearby room.
It was the club's traveling secretary. He said that Jim
Fanning, the Montreal general manager, wanted to see
me. I tossed several more coins into the pool. I remember thinking, *Three coins in the fountain. Que sera
sera. What will be will be.*

When I entered Fanning's suite, the writers were

gathered. Fanning looked up and nodded at me. He said, "Maury, you've been traded—"

In one of life's most pleasant rarities the words that I had hoped for came next.

"—to the Dodgers," Fanning said.

In his column the next day Jack Murphy, the San Diego *Union's* gifted sports editor, summed it up in a sentence: "Maury Wills was a Dodger again, and he felt complete."

It should be apparent, then, that I know about the cloud of rejection that can envelop a ballplayer who is traded and I know the joy that can accompany a trade that is satisfying. It is not a bad thing, it seems to me, for a manager to have experienced these feelings and to remember them.

8

Managers Who Can Steal a Pennant

ONCE, when he was managing the Phillies, Gene Mauch knocked the hell out of a ballplayer who had entered his dugout to make a catch—and it was all legal according to the rules. The Phils were playing New York that night, and one of the Phils had hit a foul fly that arched high toward the Philadelphia dugout. Jerry Grote, catching for the Mets, whipped off his mask, took a bead on the flight of the ball and ran toward the side of the field, stepping into the Phils' dugout.

As the ball dropped into Grote's mitt, Mauch cracked him with his arms and his body. It was a real tough shot. Grote was staggered, and he dropped the ball. Grote was so sore he couldn't see straight and was just about to tear into Mauch. Players on both sides were ready to fight. The umpires had to step in to cool the tempers.

"You son of a bitch, you can't do that to me!" Grote hollered.

"Look it up," snapped Mauch

One of the umpires did look it up. He pulled out a rule book and there it was—the rule made it clear that if an opposing player enters a dugout, he's in no-man's-land and he goes at his own risk.

"Mauch's right," the umpire said as he waved the players back to their dugouts.

Was Gene Mauch the only one on the field who knew about that rule? I'd bet on it. He was the only one with the guts to slug any player invading his dugout. As a result of Mauch's dispute with Grote, the rule was quickly changed. Now a player can go after a ball in the enemy dugout without being slugged. But not very many players even know now there is such a rule.

Scene in the Astrodome: I'm at third base for Pittsburgh. The dugout at the Astrodome is about a country mile long, with an entrance into the wooden floor close to third base. Now I knew that rule about entering a dugout, and I'd been waiting four or five years to show how smart I was.

When Bob Watson sent a pop foul into the air, I said to myself, "Hey, this is it!" I started running and didn't stop when I reached the Astros' dugout. The other players looked at me as if I were a madman. I kept going, and I had my glove in the air ready to catch the ball. Down it came—and then Jerry May, our catcher, leaned over and knocked it right out of my glove. I hadn't even seen him there, but he had come running all the way from home plate, overhustling— and spoiling my big moment. May didn't know the rule either. He thought a player was allowed to go to the edge of the dugout and lean over, like a pass receiver in football keeping his feet in bounds along the sideline. You've seen them do their little toe dance. Ballplayers do the same thing. They'll stretch into the dugout, reaching for the ball, and it hits the tip of the glove. All he had to do was take another step into the dugout, and he would have made an easy play.

Here's what the rule says: So long as you keep your

footing when you catch the ball in the dugout, the batter is out. But if you lose your footing, the ball is automatically dead. The batter's still out, but the runners each advance one base.

Anyway, Gene Mauch knew that rule—there's not a rule he doesn't know—and I rate him the smartest, the best manager in baseball today, and he could steal a pennant wherever he managed. Mauch was never rated much of a ballplayer himself, but he was always known as an outstanding competitor, a guy who could always find a way to beat you. Playing for Leo Durocher, he must have learned a lot about the game, and then he added his own knowledge. Mauch is one of the young lions, Leo, of course, being an older lion.

Until I first saw Gene Mauch, I had my own image of how a manager should look—to me a manager was potbellied, he had gray or white hair, he wore his pants down low beneath his belt, and on sunny afternoons he wore sunglasses. He always moved slowly, and when he'd sit down in the dugout, his legs would be crossed. He looked as though he had MANAGER written across his back.

Then I saw Mauch, a young guy, the first manager I ever knew who looked like an athlete. Here was a manager who ran to the mound when his pitcher was in trouble. Most managers walk out there like snails, letting the fans in the park know that they've got all the troubles in the world loaded on their backs.

Notice the next time you see a manager go to the mound. Watch how he'll get out there and then pause. You would think that when he's taking his slow walk out there, going about 100 feet, he would have mulled over his next move. But he pauses, and then he talks to the pitcher.

"How do you feel?"

"Fine, Skip."

"You tired?"

"Tired? Nah, I could throw all week if they'd get me some runs."

And on and on.

Mauch runs out there. He speaks decisively. If he wants his pitcher to stay in the game, he says a few words, pats him on the butt, and runs back to the dugout. Pitchers respect Mauch's judgment. I have never seen a pitcher come back with any static when Mauch asks for the ball. If Mauch wants that ball, the pitcher knows he's had it.

Watch Gene Mauch in the dugout some time. His eyes are constantly on the move. He's always pulling his lineup card out of his pocket, studying, figuring, scheming. Mauch is always looking ahead two, three, four innings.

Mauch is also very big on platooning his players, putting in substitutes when they're needed. Once, according to a story I heard, he was visiting his tailor in Philadelphia. When the tailor's son entered the shop, he made the introduction.

"Son, this is Mr. Gene Mauch. He manages the Expos in Montreal. But he used to manage the Phils."

The kid shook hands with Mauch and said to his father, "Does Mr. Mauch have you make all his clothes?"

"No, son, he buys some of his clothes in Montreal."

"Oh," said the kid. "You mean Mr. Mauch platoons his tailors, too?"

If you want to know how Gene Mauch stands with his peers, ask the other managers. A few years ago, before the All-Star game in Kansas City, the reporters were talking about managers with Dick Williams, then the skipper of the A's.

"If they had a baseball clinic with all the managers in the big leagues," said Williams, "I would recommend that Gene Mauch be the man who runs it. Gene's the best."

Mauch hates to lose as much as any manager I've ever known. In the '63 season his Phils were beaten by the Astros in a crucial series in September. After the final defeat Mauch stormed into the clubhouse in Houston, where the attendant had set up a fancy postgame buffet for the team. In a fury Mauch placed both hands under the long table and sent a load of Texas barbecued ribs flying in the air.

"It cost me five hundred," Mauch said later. "I had to buy new suits for Tony Gonzalez and Wes Covington."

There's nothing conventional about Gene Mauch. In the very first game in the history of the Montreal Expos we were going against the Mets. They had Tom Seaver on the mound.

Before the game Mauch said to me, "If you get to first, we'll sacrifice you over. Just this one time. Afterward you're on your own."

I was the leadoff man, and I punched a single through the infield. The next batter laid down a sacrifice bunt. The armchair strategists almost fell out of their armchairs. What the hell is this—Wills is the big base stealer, why didn't they let him steal second? Why are they pulling a sacrifice? But Mauch is shrewd. He was going after a psychological edge. He went against the book and surprised the opposition. They had to ask themselves: "What other surprises does he have up his sleeve?"

Mauch is always doing things his own way. When

he would stand up on the edge of the dugout, on the step, they called him bush. According to the book, managers are supposed to sit calmly on the bench.

They called him bush when he would root for his pitcher and against the batter. I can remember the first time I went up against the Phils when Mauch was managing the club. I thought I was a cool ballplayer, but Mauch unnerved me.

"Hit him on his ass," Mauch hollered at his pitcher. "Hit him on his legs. Spin him around!"

I went to first on a walk, stole second, and scored on a double. As I rounded home plate, I started going for the Phils' dugout. I yelled at Mauch, "Come out here. I want some of you!"

Charlie Neal pulled me back, and when I sat in our dugout, I was almost shaking with anger. Mauch's bench jockeying finally got me so flustered I went hitless the rest of the game.

"Wonder how he hits on his ass," Mauch would say in a voice loud enough for everyone to hear. He wasn't ordering his pitcher to throw a brushback, but if you were at bat, you wouldn't know that. He was yelling to make the hitter lose his composure.

Wherever Gene Mauch has managed, he's always taken inferior material and created an interesting, challenging ball club. No team has ever gone into a ball park to face a Mauch team confident of victory. Beat a Mauch team, and you know you've been in a ball game.

In '63 he took the Phillies, a nothing club, and brought them into contention. At Montreal he took charge of an expansion team composed of castoffs and minor leaguers, and he almost won it in '73. Now he is piloting the Twins.

Gene Mauch is also the toughest manager I've ever

played for in any league. This man sees everything. One time, before a game in Montreal, I was suddenly famished. I knew I had to eat something. But first I looked around for the skipper. I spotted Mauch way out in the bullpen, and I figured if he started walking now, I had almost ten minutes before he could make it into the clubhouse.

Anyone knows a ballplayer shouldn't be eating hot dogs before a ball game. But I ate one, anyway—at least I started to eat one. Just as I was taking my first bite in walked Mauch. How in the hell did he make a ten-minute walk in two minutes? How in the hell did he know I was about to indulge my appetite with a forbidden hot dog?

"Hungry, Maury?" Mauch said.

"Uh, yeah, Skip," I said.

His look was my punishment. No hot dog ever lost its flavor any quicker.

One reason Mauch is such a tremendous manager is that he knows his baseball inside and out. He knows why an error was committed, why a play didn't work. And he's a man who runs his own ball club. Mauch would never turn to one of his coaches and say, "Use your own judgment."

Mauch also knows more facets of the game than any manager I've ever seen. With the Dodgers I was always the one who gave the lectures at training camp on baserunning and stealing. When I went to the Pirates, I was still the teacher. But with the Expos it was Mauch who taught my specialty, and I listened and even picked up a few pointers.

What I like about Mauch is that he has an original baseball mind. He was the first manager to bring in a five-man infield. This one had everybody in the ball park buzzing. It went like this. Let's say it's the ninth inning, there are less than two outs, and the opposing team has the winning run on third base. It's a road game, which means that the other club goes to bat last. Now if the batter hits a long fly to the outfield, the run scores. Or if he gets the hit, that's the ball game. Something else can beat you—a ground ball through the infield.

One night in Philadelphia Mauch faced this situation, and here's how he handled it. He brought two of his outfielders about 100 feet closer to the infield grass. One of his outfielders he stationed near the shortstop, and that gave him protection, one extra man's worth, against a ball hit to the infield. It was a gamble, and it worked—the batter grounded out.

Mauch was the first manager to come up with what's called a double move. This one is tricky. I'll explain it step by step. Your pitcher is in trouble. He's batting ninth in the order, of course. Your hitter in the eighth slot has just made the last out of the inning. This means the pitcher will be leading off the next inning.

Here's where the double move comes in. You put in a new pitcher, and at the same time you substitute another player, who goes in as the ninth batter in the order. The new pitcher goes into the lineup batting eighth.

Now the inning rolls around, and it's time for your club to bat. Who's up first? Not the pitcher. He's batting eighth. Your other player, the substitute, goes up first, being the ninth man in the order. So the pitcher doesn't come to bat until eight men have come up before him, and by then maybe your club has picked up some runs.

Mauch pulled this one in the mid-sixties. Baseball

men had to see it in operation three or four times before it was accepted as sound strategy. Now it's the going thing, a touch of Mauch that spread around the league.

Here's another example of Mauch strategy at work. This one came about at a blackboard session in spring training when I was with Montreal. It's an offensive play, and Mauch, smart tactician that he is, also gave us the defensive counterplay. As Mauch outlined the moves on the blackboard, I kept looking for flaws, and I couldn't find any. I still can't.

The play made a big impression on me. Later that season, when I was traded back to the Dodgers, I explained it to Walt Alston. I said, "Mauch is going to use it if he gets a chance, and I've got the defense for it, too."

Alston hustled me up before the club at a pregame meeting. "Maury's got a play he wants to tell you about," he said.

"Okay," I said, "we've got runners on first and third, less than two outs. Somebody hits a foul back at the screen, and their catcher gets it. The runner at first tags up and breaks for second. The catcher has got to make a long throw from the screen."

"That throw's a bitch," said Tom Haller, our catcher.

"And then," I went on, "the guy on third comes right in. It's like a double steal. If the catcher doesn't throw, the runner on first has an easy way to second. Now if the first baseman has to go to the dugout for a foul pop, he's the guy that has the long throw. If he makes the throw to second, the guy at third scores. Or if it's the third baseman who catches the foul pop on the other side, the guy on first breaks for second, and there's a chance of the runner at third scoring."

"Let's go back to the catcher," Haller said.

"The catcher," I said, "has to eat the goddamn ball."

The play wasn't all that unfamiliar to the Dodgers. We had a play in the same situation where the catcher throws the ball about a foot over the pitcher's head. The pitcher reaches up, grabs the ball and becomes the cutoff man to nab the runner if he goes for home.

But Mauch's defense was better. As I explained to the Dodgers that day, Mauch prefers the shortstop as the cutoff man, and he should come in about halfway between the mound and second base.

The next time we played the Expos, in Dodger Stadium, they had runners on first and third. A Montreal player hit a pop foul that went up near the back of the net. Tom Haller moved under the ball. I charged in; the second baseman moved over to cover the bag. Haller caught the ball and threw it to me. I spun around and glanced at the runner on first—he hadn't moved. But the runner at third had started for home.

I could feel it in my bones—Mauch's own play was just about to backfire on him. So I threw the ball to Bill Sadakis at third. But Bill was staring down at Haller, my throw went past him, and the runner went on home. In other words, we had the right strategy, but we didn't execute. Score one for Gene Mauch.

There's more to Gene Mauch than strategy. He's a manager with some feeling for his ballplayers. In the spring of '74 the Expos were scheduled to fly down to San Juan, Puerto Rico, for two exhibition games. They were set for a time before the squad was cut, and Mauch was told he could only take twenty-five players. Among the players not included was Jose Morales, a native of Puerto Rico, with a family in San Juan: Morales pleaded with Mauch to be allowed to go with the team.

Morales is a marginal player, and Mauch knew that when the season began, he wouldn't be wearing a Montreal uniform. He also knew what a trip to Puerto Rico meant to him. Mauch solved the problem his own way. He left another player, a non-Latin, at home and Jose Morales saw his family in Puerto Rico.

I've listened to Mauch talk about his philosophy of baseball. It goes something like this: "You put things to a test. You yell at the other ball club. If your razzing gets them down, keep at it. If the razzing stimulates them, zip it. You play away from their strength and go to their weakness. To hell with the past. Each game is a new book. Each situation is a new book."

Mauch would say, "My whole theory of managing a ball club can be summed up in one sentence: Whatever you think is necessary, do it. One of the big things is knowing the rules. I've had as much fun reading a rulebook as some of my players have drooling over *Playboy*.

"Sometimes you play it straight, sometimes you gamble. You do whatever is necessary. Managing a ball club narrows down to this: Either you have a feel for the game and the personality for it, or you don't. If you do, you manage. If you don't, you take a hike."

Running as an entry with Mauch, Billy Martin is another manager who could steal a pennant. In some ways, Martin and Mauch are similar. Much of what I have to say about Billy Martin has to be based on hearsay, but I like what I've heard from the players. Martin treats his players as he wanted to be treated in his own playing days. He's not one of those managers who have MANAGER written in invisible ink across his back. He's never forgotten that he was a ballplayer himself.

Billy has his own rules. Once, when he was managing the Minnesota Twins, he caught two players coming back to the hotel long after curfew. Actually, they came in at the same time that Billy did. Billy said to them, "What do you want me to do—do you want to be fined or would you rather buy me a dozen golf balls?"

One of the guys said, "Skip, what kind of ball do you use?"

As Billy puts it, "I check the cliques. I check the alibiers. I watch the clock punchers. I want to keep the guys happy, but a manager doesn't have to be soft."

At spring training Martin drums the fundamentals into his club, whether he's dealing with rookies or veterans. He participates in everything, and he sets a frantic pace. He'll warm up with his players in an exercise session. Then he'll go from group to group, telling them how he wants things done. He's big on base stealing, how to take a lead, how to work the suicide squeeze. Billy is the exact opposite of some of the managers I've seen who give the players some bats and balls and tell them to go out and practice.

Billy is the type of manager who leads his team. He's not a guy to stand around and hope for something good to happen. He's got signs for everybody on the club—he'll shoot a sign to his catcher for a pitchout, for instance—and they have to stay alert and watch him in the dugout.

I don't think it's any fluke that Martin can take average teams and put them into contention. Maybe he'll get into a few fights along the way—Billy's been known to punch a guy's lights out—but he'll have his ball club hustling from the minute it reports to camp. Bill can do anything but get along with his bosses. He's had run-ins with Calvin Griffith at Minnesota, with Jim Campbell at Detroit. But those two are strictly Establishment baseball men. Their idea of a manager is somebody who doesn't make waves. Now Billy's managing the Yankees, back where he once played.

It's true that Billy doesn't have the sweetest disposition in the world. As an NBC broadcaster I heard about one incident that turned Billy off, and we almost lost him for interviews. It's a rule at NBC that the network pays ballplayers $50 for an on-camera interview. Managers are expected to do an interview on TV without getting paid.

One of the unit men supervised an interview with Billy, and then he slipped him $10. Billy raised hell and threw the money back at him. Some managers might have said, "Thanks," and bought cigars for the clubhouse attendants or put the money in a fund for a players' party. Billy was so angry he told NBC he would never be interviewed again by anybody from the network.

In 1973, my rookie year on TV, I told the crew I wanted to do an interview with Billy Martin. They told me that he'd throw me out of the clubhouse. But I decided I'd take a chance. I went in, with a microphone in my hand. A camera crew followed me.

Billy looked up, and he couldn't believe what he saw. I didn't let him say a word. "Before you say anything, Skip, I know what happened before," I said. Then I went into a fast sales pitch about all the fans out in televisionland who wanted to hear his opinions.

Billy got up. "Okay," he said, "but make it fast."

Maybe Billy just wanted to get rid of me the easiest

way. Or maybe he was being nice to an old ballplayer. Either way I didn't much care. I got my interview, and I felt as proud as if I'd stolen a base on Warren Spahn.

So those are my two top managers—Gene Mauch and Billy Martin—and now they're both managing in the same league. In a way, it's a shame. I would have liked to have seen them in opposing leagues, going at each other in a World Series. What a World Series that would have been—manager versus manager, as well as team against team. Mauch and Martin would be calling every play, using strategy every minute, pulling the unexpected.

With such a World Series, the fans might have seen baseball the way it was meant to be played—and you can bet it wouldn't have been baseball by the book.

9

Leo

IF a genie in a bottle could give me a choice of witnessing any event in history, I might pick the clubhouse of the New York Giants on the afternoon of October 3, 1957. On that day, in the last half of the ninth inning of the final game of the National League playoffs, Bobby Thomson cracked the home run that destroyed the Brooklyn Dodgers, 5–4, to win the pennant for Leo Durocher's Giants. They still call it the Miracle of Coogan's Bluff.

Afterward it was bedlam in the Giants' clubhouse. I'd like to have been there to see Leo, a smile on his face and a glass of champagne in his hand, answering questions from the press.

In all seriousness one of the writers asked, "Leo, what was the turning point of the game?"

Faced with a question of such numbing denseness, for the first time in his life Leo "The Lip" Durocher was speechless! And that was the second historic event of the day.

Leo was always known as one of baseball's great nonstop free-style talkers. But that's only one side of the man. Leo Durocher is the best cardplayer, the best pool player, the best dresser, the most dynamic, the most interesting, the most unforgettable character I ever met in my baseball career—and he was also the smartest manager the game has ever known.

"Nice guys finish last," Leo once said. And he used to say, "On the field I come to kill you. After the game I'll buy you dinner, but on the field I come to kill you."

There was another Durocher saying: "I'd trip my mother to win a ball game. I'd help her up, brush her off, tell her I'm sorry—but *Mother don't make it to third!*"

I played for a lot of managers in my time. It's a big regret in my career that I never played on a team managed by Leo Durocher. The closest I came was in the early 1960s, when Leo was hired as a coach of the Los Angeles Dodgers, an aide to manager Walt Alston.

Leo came to the Dodgers under unusual circumstances. He was living in Beverly Hills, temporarily out of baseball. General manager Buzzie Bavasi met with him one day.

As Buzzie tells it, Leo was downcast.

"Buzzie," Leo said, "I'm being blackballed from baseball. I can't get a job. Nobody wants me."

"That's not true," Buzzie told him. "What's true is that you've priced yourself out of the market. That's why nobody wants to offer you a job and have you turn it down."

"Well, I've always come high," Leo admitted. "But I can't sit around. I've got to do something in baseball. It's my life."

"All right," Buzzie said, "would you coach for twenty-three thousand dollars?"

"Hell, yes," Leo said. And he was hired.

When the appointment was announced to the press, Buzzie had a specific point to make.

"I want this clearly understood," Buzzie told the reporters. "As long as I'm the general manager of the Los Angeles Dodgers, Leo Durocher will never manage this ball club. He's here as a coach and only a coach. There will be no trouble on that score between Leo Durocher and Walt Alston. If there's any trouble, it can only be caused by what you people write. It's all up to you."

Buzzie always had a soft spot for Leo Durocher, going back to his days with the Brooklyn Dodgers when Leo was the manager. One of Buzzie's favorite stories concerns the time just before World War II when the draft was being put into effect.

Buzzie was in his office filling out a government form about Leo's draft status. Leo and several players were also in his office.

Before writing in the space under "profession," Buzzie deliberated. He decided that "baseball manager" didn't sound official enough. He chose to use the phrase "director of athletics."

"Hey," Buzzie called out, "how do you spell 'athletics'?"

One of the players said, "You spell it a-t-h-l-e-t-i-c-k-s."

"Yeah, that's right," Leo said.

But Leo wasn't paid to win spelling bees.

Napoleon had his Elba, when he was between conquests. LA was Leo's Elba. He felt that he was between manager's jobs.

It would be hard to pick two men of more opposite natures than Leo Durocher and Walt Alston, and in spite of Bavasi's announcement to the press, they had their differences. Walt Alston is a big, bulky country type of man with a slow pace. Some of the press called him the farmer behind his back. Leo was slicker, the big-city swinger, the sharp dresser. Even back in the twenties, Leo's New York Yankee teammates called him Fifth Avenue.

The first time I saw Leo Durocher is still imprinted in my mind, like a tattoo. It was in Vero Beach, Florida, at the Dodgertown training camp. The sky was bright and blue, decorated with a few cumulus clouds, the beginning of a typically warm and humid Florida day. There was Leo, the new coach, standing along first base talking. He was already the center of attention. He was surrounded by sportswriters, photographers, tourists, kids. All told, there must have been about 150 people gathered around him. Even if you didn't know who he was, you would have to guess that he was somebody special.

"That's Leo," I whispered to Jim Gilliam as we took our positions in the infield.

"Damned if it ain't," Jim said. "That's Leo!"

Leo walked over to the right of home plate—he had a strutting king-of-the-hill stride as though he had just bought the ball park—and he picked up a baseball and a fungo bat.

"Okay, Alice!" he barked at me. The man had a voice like a Klaxon.

Then he hit the meanest ground ball any coach had ever hit to me in a practice session. I fielded it cleanly and whipped it to first. Damn, I felt proud of myself.

"Okay, Susie!" Leo yelled. Now he was talking to Jim Gilliam at third base. Crack! Another sizzling grounder, hard and mean.

"Here's one for you, Mabel!"

This time Leo was talking to the second baseman, Charlie Neal. It was Leo's way, calling the players by girls' names, challenging us to play like men. And we all wanted to do our best and look good for him.

We all loved the way he created excitement. If any

other coach hit balls at us even half that hard, we'd
have complained, "Come on, Coach, let up." But Leo
made us rise to the bait. He was an expert with a fungo
bat. He had a way of making his bat hit the bottom of
the ball, cutting it, giving it a reverse spin, and that
made it tough as hell to catch.

Among the Dodger players there was a feeling that
Leo was more of a Dodger than most of us could ever
hope to be. To us, he was Mr. Dodger in the way that
Ernie Banks was Mr. Cub. Leo had been a Dodger
ballplayer and a Dodger manager when we were kids.
He had been away, and now he was back where he belonged, in a Dodger uniform. Maybe Leo didn't feel
that way. He wasn't much for sentiment.

Leo was a famous part of baseball history. Bud
Shrake of *Sports Illustrated* summed it up, years later,
when he wrote, "Before this country had ever heard of
Kennedy, Nixon, Gable, Disney, Earhart, DiMaggio,
Presley, Flash Gordon or Dr. Spock, people knew
about Leo."

It wasn't easy separating fact from legend, but we
had heard quite a bit about Leo Ernest Durocher. He
had come up to the major leagues as a switch-hitting
shortstop to play for the old Yankees, in the 1920s. The
story was that Babe Ruth himself used to drive him to
Yankee Stadium in his Packard roadster. Leo was the
only ballplayer I ever heard of who had played polo.
He then became a member of the famous Gas House
Gang, the St. Louis Cardinals of the 1930s, playing
with Dizzy Dean and Frankie Frisch and Ducky Med-
wick. As a manager he had led the Dodgers and then
the Giants to pennants. He had been like a father to
Willie Mays, and he was a buddy to celebrities like
Frank Sinatra and Danny Kaye. But the most impor-

tant thing was baseball knowledge seemed to flow from the man's pores.

He was always a cocky son of a bitch, but never afraid to admit his mistakes. When Leo was the captain of the St. Louis Cardinals, he was introduced at a baseball dinner by Branch Rickey with these words: "And now I give you the captain of the team, a man with an infinite capacity for making a bad situation worse." Then he pointed to Leo, who sat there and grinned and nodded.

This was the man who had been suspended by Commissioner Happy Chandler for an entire season because it was said that he knew some disreputable characters. Hell, Leo knew everybody, from the top of the social scale to the bottom. You couldn't expect him to ask everybody he met for his or her pedigree.

No one in baseball had a bigger reputation for baiting umpires. But in his later years I think Leo would go after an umpire because he knew the fans expected it of him. He gave them the show they came to see. The fans came out to the park to watch Sandy Koufax pitch strikeouts. They wanted to see me steal bases. They'd be disappointed if Leo didn't get into a scrape with an umpire and start a shin-kicking contest.

Even if we were winning, after too many peaceful innings, Leo would say, "Got to straighten him out." Then he'd go out after an umpire. He had his own way of doing that, too. Leo would always maneuver so that he would face the field and the umpire had to face the stands. In that way, Leo's words wouldn't be heard by the fans but instead would carry to the outfield.

Sometimes Leo would invite trouble. At other times trouble would come to him. Once, in Los Angeles, he had just left the stadium and was going to his car, signing autographs for the kids as he walked. When he arrived at his car, he said, "That's it, kids. Gotta go now."

In this crowd of kids, a man held up a pen and a scorecard. "Sign this, Leo," he ordered.

Leo ignored him and opened his car door and settled into the driver's seat. The guy started rapping hard at his window and swearing at him. That's all that Leo needed. He flung the door open.

"Take your best shot, friend," Leo said. The guy swung. Leo stepped aside and hit back. With one punch Leo decked him and broke the stranger's jaw.

Later he brought Leo into court. Maybe this is typical of Los Angeles or of Leo's fame, but it was the only courtroom session I ever heard of that was broadcast live on the radio.

The judge said, "But, Leo, this man only weighs one hundred twenty pounds."

Leo said, "Hell, Judge, I didn't bring my scales."

The judge laughed and threw the case out of court.

To see Leo on or off the field was to behold the complete fashion plate. I can't ever remember seeing a wrinkle in either Leo's street clothes or his baseball uniform. He looked as though he stood up all the time.

Someone once said about Joe DiMaggio that wherever he sits, it's the head of the table. It was like that with Leo and his clothes. Leo's clothes may not have conformed to the style of the day, but whatever he wore, he was always in the height of fashion. For instance, when some of the players started wearing boots to be in style, Leo still wore his loafers, and they were always shined, and his heels were always squared off as though they had just come fresh from the cobbler's bench.

We envied Leo's style, and we tried to imitate him, but he was inimitable. He had charisma before anyone knew what the hell it was. After a game we would watch him standing in front of the mirror, carefully combing his few remaining strands of chestnut brown hair. He always smelled of the most expensive cologne. Even during a game his fingernails were neatly manicured. He was the first man in baseball I ever saw with polish on his nails.

He never seemed to need a shave. Even when he would start to shave, always with a brand-new blue-blade in his razor, his skin looked as smooth as a baby's rump. He'd shave with slow, deliberate strokes, and he'd be saying to nobody in particular, "I'm in a hurry. Got to see Frank for dinner."

He meant Frank Sinatra. Leo was always talking about Frank Sinatra, partly because he was proud of his close friendship, but also, I think, because he knew we liked to hear him. We got a kick out of him saying, "I saw Frank last week at the Springs." Not even the rawest rookie had to ask who Frank was.

When he finished dressing, Leo would go to the clubhouse attendant to pick up his valuables. We'd watch him as he would insert his Parliaments in his gold cigarette holder—probably a gift from Frank—and slip a gold ring on his pinky finger, and pocket his wallet, which always contained two or three thousand dollars. And off he would go, in his new Lincoln Continental, into the night.

Leo is the only baseball man I ever knew who had his uniform tailor-made, and nobody ever looked more born to a major-league uniform. He was the first man to wear his belt buckle slightly off to the right for a rakish touch. It was one of his trademarks. He wore his baseball cap at a right angle, and this gave him the look of a riverboat gambler with three aces in his hand.

His baseball shoes were always shined with shoe polish. This may not sound important, but since a ball club's baseball shoes have to be cleaned and shined every day, the clubhouse man uses some kind of gummy substance, going over all the shoes in line with a paint brush.

But not for Leo. He insisted on a true shine for his shoes. They were soft-leather Spalding Dot shoes, and they must have been at least thirty years old. They couldn't be duplicated anywhere. Those shoes of Leo's belonged in the Hall of Fame.

As a base stealer I was particularly interested in shoes and feet. There's a theory in sports that the bigger the feet, the better the athlete. It sounds logical since the feet take such a beating in most sports. Ballplayers generally wear spikes one size smaller than their street shoes. Sandy Koufax, for instance, wore a size 12 spike and a 13D street shoe. I wear a 10D-wide street shoe and a 9½ spike.

I was always experimenting with my baseball shoes. During a season I would alternate between ten pairs of spikes. In 1962 I had the idea of taking out the inner soles in the hope of gaining a split second in speed. Shoes were damned important to me.

I asked Leo if I could make a pattern of his shoes, and I sent them to Japan. The Japanese shoemaker sent back two pairs of shoes modeled after his. They were good shoes, but they weren't quite like Leo's.

I showed them to Leo, and he inspected them closely. Then he shook his head. "Maury," he said, "there's nothing like an original."

Leo was an original. This is something the fans sensed about him. He was the only manager, and I'm including Casey Stengel, that the fans specifically came out to see. In the newer ball parks they have electronic scoreboards for messages, and they use it to advertise future home games. It might say: HANK AARON AND THE BRAVES THIS WEEKEND. When Leo was managing the Cubs and, later, the Astros, he's the one who would be the drawing card. LEO DUROCHER AND HIS CUBS NEXT, it might say on the scoreboard. Or LEO DU-ROCHER AND HIS ASTROS. Was any other manager given that kind of distinction? I don't think so.

When he was managing, Leo used to say, "If anybody's out after hours, I'll catch him 'cause I'm out a little myself." But he was always understanding of his players. If he looked into a cocktail lounge and saw some of his men at the bar, he would walk in and say, "Hiya, fellas." Then to the bartender: "Set up a round for everybody." Nobody else ever picked up a tab when Leo was around.

On the road, between paychecks on the first and fifteenth of the month, a player might run into a bad case of the shorts. He knew that he could turn to Leo.

"How much you need, kid?" Leo would say, pulling out his fat wallet.

"Fifty would help. Pay you when we get home. Thanks, Leo."

Leo would wave his hand in the air. "Forget it, kid."

Once, on a cold spring day in Chicago, we were shivering in the dugout as the wind zipped in from Lake Michigan. Leo went into the clubhouse, brewed a pot of coffee, and brought out the cups.

"Hey, Leo," somebody said, "this tastes good. It warms you up."

Leo smiled. "It should," he said. "Brandy does good things for coffee."

He especially liked ballplayers who attacked the

game as he did, with fire and zest. Once I remember hearing him refer to Jackie Robinson as "a Durocher with talent." A fighter himself, he sympathized with the problems of the black player. In the 1950s, managing the Giants, he would play cards with the black players, talk with them, eat with them, go out with them.

There was another knack that Leo had, whether he was dealing with blacks or whites. In baseball, it is traditional for players to be called by their last names— it's Koufax, Drysdale, Davis, Wills. Leo was different. He would call us by our given names—it was always Sandy, Don, Willie, Maury. For a man known for his gruffness, this always seemed to me a nice touch. It was Leo's way of saying that he regarded his players not just as last names in a lineup but as human beings.

Leo had the touch, and he also had a flair for the dramatic gesture. In September, 1963, we were in St. Louis for a crucial series with the Cardinals. We were in first place, the Cards in second, one game behind. The atmosphere had nearly all the tension of a World Series. We won the first two games. Before the third and final game Leo stood up in the clubhouse.

"Listen," he hollered, "we win it, and it's golf shoes for everybody!"

We won the game. A week later we were home in Los Angeles, and some delivery guy comes into the Dodgers' clubhouse pushing two wheelbarrows. They were filled with Footjoy golf shoes that must have cost about $30 apiece. Leo had bought shoes for the players, the coaches, the batboys, the trainer, the clubhouse attendants—thirty-five pairs of golf shoes. It cost him a bundle.

Leo beamed. "You guys came through," he said. "I come through."

As rough as he was with men, Leo was courtly and elegant with women. They loved him, and Leo returned the compliment. You might see him in the clubhouse, hollering and agitating. A minute later he would be on the field, all charm and smiles, in the presence of women visitors.

He had once won the pool championship of southern Ohio, and he could handle a stick like a professional. At Dodgertown one hot spring night, we were playing rise and fly pool, which means that when you lose a game you give up the cue. Leo strolled in.

"Here, Leo, take my stick," someone said. He nodded and carefully set his jacket on the back of a nearby chair. He was the only one at camp who wore a jacket on a hot night. Then he cleared the table, clicking off his shots with precision and authority. He was standing at the table, waiting for another challenger, when I spotted Walt Alston at the door.

Now Walt Alston was a super pool player, and there was nothing the players wanted more than to see the two of them, Alston and Durocher, the skipper and the coach, going head to head. I went to the door.

"Skip," I said, "come on in, shoot some pool."

He could see Leo alone at the table, and he sensed what was happening. He hesitated. But I led him on.

"Leo, we got a match for you," I yelled.

Durocher was leaning over the table, touching up his cue tip with resin. "I'll take anybody," Leo said, without looking up. "Name him—Willie Mosconi, Minnesota Fats. . . ."

Then his eyes shot up, and he saw Walt Alston.

For a second he hesitated. But there was no turning back. A crowd gathered around the table. Someone put a stick in Alston's hand. We racked up the balls and the match was on.

It was like the scene in the movie *The Hustler*, in that the pool game was a reflection of something deeper, a testing of character between two men of strong wills and different personalities. Besides, there had always been an undercurrent of dislike between the manager and his coach.

It was a meeting of the lion, meaning Leo, of course, and the ox, which was the way I saw Walt Alston. The lion is flamboyant and vocal. The ox is steady, durable, plodding along slowly but forever.

On this steamy Florida night the tension began to build. The match began in silence. Alston had the first shot, and he was hot. He couldn't miss.

"Hey, Leo," one of the players cracked, "you're losin'."

Leo glowered. He hates to lose. Whenever he would ever start to lose at anything, his personality quickly changed. His charm would recede. He stood with his arms folded in front of him, his expression morose, staring at Alston making shot after shot. Then Alston missed after running up two racks.

We could razz Leo, but it was different with the skipper. When Alston missed a shot, we didn't say a word. Now it was Leo's turn, and he came back to life. It was fascinating to watch his transformation. He started clicking with his cue, rattling off shot after shot until he had put in two racks. Then he missed. But when either of these top-level players missed a shot, they would play defensive pool, leaving the other with a close to impossible shot. They were like pros, going at each other in dead silence.

It was a contest that neither man had wanted to start and neither wanted to finish, whatever the outcome. Then, with the score even, Alston suddenly put down his cue and glanced at his watch.

"Staff meeting at eight thirty," Alston announced.

Was it a welcome ruse by Alston or was there actually a staff meeting that night on the manager's schedule? We'll never know. Alston quickly walked out the door.

A moment later Leo laid his cue in the rack. He put on his jacket. Then he strutted out the door. We knew there would never be a rematch of the lion and the ox.

"Nice guys finish last," Leo had said back in 1946, referring to Mel Ott, then the Giants' manager. The phrase has long been misinterpreted. What Leo meant was that a leader can't win without toughness of character, and he won't win if he's unable to instill his own burning determination in his players.

It's true that many people disliked Leo. He could be grumpy and tactless, and his remarks were often cutting. But in terms of his kindness to younger players, the compassion he gave to black players, his capacity for friendship, and the generosity of his spirit, Leo Durocher was surely one of the nice guys of baseball.

And he did finish last. But just once.

10

Walt

ONE night in the spring of '74 Jimmy Wynn tore loose with three home runs for the Dodgers against the San Diego Padres. For Walt Alston, the Dodger manager, the event brought back some memories. As he recalled to the writers later, Alston had once hit three home runs in one game himself while he was playing first base and managing the Springfield, Ohio, club in the Middle Atlantic League. That had been more than thirty years before, but Walt remembered it well.

"Not many people noticed," Walt said. "I hit my three homers on the same day my pitcher threw a nohitter. When I read the papers the next morning, the only place I could find my name was in the box score."

Somehow, that incident seemed to fit the image that Walter Emmons Alston has presented all through the years. He gets the job done in almost an anonymous way. As a ballplayer Walt spent just about all his career in the minors. He went up to bat only once in the big leagues, with the St. Louis Cardinals. He was a pinch hitter, and he struck out.

Unlike most managers you might name, Walt Alston could have made his living in other ways than baseball. He holds a bachelor of science degree from Miami University of Ohio—Paul Brown, the football coach, was a few classes ahead of him—and he could have gone into college coaching. He could have taught high school science. He could have been a furniture designer—he made most of the furniture in his home at Darrtown, the small town in Ohio where he was born and still lives. He could have been a terrific pool hustler.

Instead, he chose a career in baseball. He's spent more than twenty years now managing the Dodgers. Only Connie Mack, who led the Philadelphia Athletics for fifty years, and John McGraw, thirty-one years with the New York Giants, have enjoyed a longer time with one club. And you have to remember that Connie Mack had some influence with management—he owned the ball club.

Try to consider Walt Alston in this context: In the 1954 season, when he came to the Dodgers, the other managers in the National League were Charlie Grimm, Stan Hack, Terry Moore, Fred Haney, Birdie Tebbetts, Eddie Stanky, and Leo Durocher. Only Alston is still active as a manager.

The man who preceded Alston with the Dodgers, Charlie Dressen, was fired for an unusual reason—he wrote a letter, or his wife did, demanding a two-year contract. Alston must have learned from this error, and he's gone, season after season, with a one-year contract. "That fellow," Casey Stengel once said about Walt, "has worked twenty years on a one-year contract. You've got to figure the Dodgers are satisfied with their manager."

I called him Skip, just as most ballplayers say when they're addressing the manager. Alston's old nickname is Smokey. This goes back to when he was a kid in high school, and he had a fastball that used to smoke past the hitters. But Alston never liked being called

Smokey. I like the idea of calling a manager Skip. It falls easily off the tongue. In the colleges and the pros, football players usually call their head man Coach. It's a title, like Professor or Doctor. But in baseball we couldn't very well call the boss Manager. It wouldn't sound right. So he's Skip.

Now for the crunch question: How good a manager is Walter Alston? What kind of man is he? These aren't easy questions to answer.

I'll begin by saying that Alston has fooled a lot of the doubters just by being the Dodger manager all these years. When Alston was given the job in the fall of 1953, one of the New York writers slipped it to him with this: "The Dodgers do not need a manager and that is why they got Alston." What he meant by that was—besides giving Alston the shiv—is that the Dodgers were so loaded with talent in the Jackie Robinsons, the Duke Sniders, the Carl Furillos, the Roy Campanellas, the Don Newcombes that they only needed somebody who could write the names in a lineup and hand the card to the umpire.

They used to call him the Pebble Thrower because he'd stand up in the dugout and toss pebbles in the air. But he won pennants. Could we have won more? I'll put that another way: *Should* we have won more under Walt Alston? My answer to that is, yes, we should have, considering the talent we had.

Alston won with a team of sluggers in Brooklyn in the fifties, and he won with a team that had speed and cunning and pitching in the sixties. And he won with a lot of second-guessing from the general manager, Buzzie Bavasi. But it was Bavasi, an astute baseball man, who saved Alston's job when our club fell apart in the last week of the 1962 season.

"I owe Bavasi an awful lot," Alston has said, "which is why I don't mind stories about his criticism of me during some losing ball games. But, shucks, why shouldn't a general manager have second-guessing privileges?"

He really does say "shucks," but Walt Alston can express himself with a lot stronger language when he wants to. One time he exploded with a blazing flurry of words at Leo Durocher, who was then coaching for him. We had a very incongruous situation with Alston as the manager and Leo Durocher as one of his coaches. Leo is a born leader, and there's no way he's going to accept being second-in-command.

One night in Pittsburgh we were in the dugout, and Leo started complaining about Ron Fairly, our first baseman, missing a sign.

Leo was saying things like: "If I were the manager of this ball club, I'd fine the son of a bitch."

As Leo well knew, Alston could hear every word. This was about three months into the season, and Alston had already had about enough of Leo's comments. Skip took two steps toward him, and he looked Leo right in the eye. Alston's a big man—6 feet 2 inches and well over 200 pounds. Leo goes around 5 feet 9.

"I am tired of your shit," Alston said.

We all gaped in disbelief. Then Alston walked away, stopped, and turned around to face Leo again.

"You do the coaching, and I'll do the managing," Alston said to Leo. "I'll fine whoever I want to fine on this ball club. Now is that understood?"

Leo clenched his teeth. It was one of the few times that I ever saw Leo Durocher even slightly cowed.

At one point near the end of the '64 season Walt had

some trouble with outfielder Tommy Davis. Word had got back to Alston that Tommy was out dancing on the night after he said he couldn't play ball because his leg hurt. Alston was furious. The next day Alston and Davis almost got into a punching match, but the players broke it up.

A few days later Tommy was complaining because Alston had laid a $100 fine on him. The skipper came back with a warning. "That kind of talk will cost you an extra hundred dollars," Alston told him. He bit off the words like chunks off a ripe red apple.

Davis kept sounding off. "Dammit, Skip, what right have you got to take my money?"

Alston said, "If that's how you want it, it's now three hundred. You want to go for four?"

Davis mumbled something about being hit in the wallet and walked off.

Alston could scare people. One night in spring training Sandy Koufax and Larry Sherry, who were roommates, sneaked in after curfew. They thought they had made it safely and locked the door. But Alston had heard them, and he started pounding on the door. He hit that door so hard he shattered his World Series ring. In fact, he broke the door down, and Koufax and Sherry stood there, terrified, in front of him. Alston gave them an ass chewing you wouldn't believe. He woke up the whole training camp. Hell, he must have awakened the entire state of Florida.

I remember one time in Pittsburgh when we were all grumbling about the team bus that was taking us to the airport from Forbes Field. That was some bus! It was more like the trolley on *Petticoat Junction*. It was old with hard backs and cramped and no air conditioning.

Pittsburgh has so many hills to negotiate, and this old crate would sputter and moan, and we'd have to move to the side of the road to allow the cars to pass us.

We had just lost a doubleheader to the Pirates. As players we felt that comfortable transportation was necessary to console us. The Pirates, meanwhile, had a spacious, air-conditioned bus. They were headed for a road trip, which meant we were both going out to the airport at about the same time. The Pittsburgh bus passed us on a hill, and the Pirates waved and made faces and jeered and hollered witty remarks, like "Get a horse!"

Alston was seated in the manager's spot near the driver. He could hear every word of our complaining, and it grated on his patience. He wasn't feeling too cheerful after losing two games either.

Finally, he had enough. "Pull over," he told the driver. "Stop the goddamn bus."

The silence that now hung like a heavy cloud was broken by Alston's voice. "Shut the hell up," Alston said. "I don't want to hear one more word about this bus. If anybody on this ball club wants to dispute me and talk about this goddamn bus, I'll be waiting outside."

The skipper motioned the driver to open the door, and he stepped outside and waited, his arms folded in front of him.

Alston was challenging us, physically, and there was no response. It should have been funny, one man standing up against a busful of ballplayers, but it wasn't funny to us. Who would want to take on a man who had beaten big Frank Howard—6 feet 6 and 240 pounds—at baseball's version of arm wrestling? In fact, when Alston made his stand in the bus, he was staring right at Frank Howard. He was making it clear that he was ready to take on the biggest man first.

None of us moved. Alston returned to his seat. "All right," he said to the driver, "take us to the airport."

There's a sequel to the story. The next time we were in Pittsburgh, we had moved up in class—to a big, spacious, air-conditioned bus, and we had no more scenes out of *High Noon*.

I have always had the feeling that Walt Alston never felt completely relaxed and at home as the Dodger manager until after the late sixties. By then he knew he had made it. The coaches who might have been a threat to his job were gone—Charlie Dressen, Leo Durocher, Bobby Bragan, Preston Gomez, all had moved on. And of course, the players from the Brooklyn days were long since gone. Jim Gilliam, the infielder, came in later, and he's the only one left, as Alston's coach.

It's no secret that when Alston was first called up by the Brooklyn Dodgers, to many of the players he was strictly a minor leaguer. They didn't think he had much spark. Mostly they thought he was indecisive.

In one game they tell about, the bases were loaded, and Alston came out to the mound to talk with his pitcher, catcher, and infielders.

"Um, what do you think we should do?" Alston said.

"You're the manager," Jackie Robinson snapped. "You get paid for it. You tell us."

But the old Dodgers learned to respect him physically. There was the time in Brooklyn that Alston ordered Don Newcombe, one of his top pitchers, into his office. Earlier, in the clubhouse, Newcombe had said something derogatory about Alston as a manager. Alston locked the door and dropped the key in his pocket. Then he faced Newcombe. Verbal or physical, he was putting out a challenge. The next move was up to the big pitcher. Newcombe listened meekly while Alston laid down the law.

Later Alston had to take part in one of baseball's most difficult periods, the transition from one set of players to another. When one generation of ballplayers has to give way to the next, it's never easy for anyone, including the manager. It's like a relay team, with each runner handing the baton to the next—except that in baseball it doesn't work that way. In baseball, it's not so graceful. When an older player hands the baton to the younger player, he'll try to make him drop it or make it look as though he dropped it.

Tommy Davis, for example, was taking over from Wally Moon, who had won the LA fans with his Moon Shot home runs over the short Coliseum wall. Wally Moon was one of the rare ballplayers. A quiet man, he sat on the bench and never complained—at least out loud—as his job was being taken from him.

At center field Willie Davis was moving in to replace Duke Snider, who became bitter and sour. Duke was like a great, proud warrior who hated the fact that he finally had to turn in his shield. I was succeeding Don Zimmer, and he did his share of understandable griping.

All down the line, the new was replacing the old, and Walt Alston was in charge and had to live through it and still win.

It's hard to say just how much a manager contributes to a ball club's success or failure. It must be something that can be measured. Otherwise, why have a manager? Leadership is one of those rare qualities. As a musician once told me, the world is divided into a very few leaders and a lot of sidemen, which is the musicians' word for other musicians in the band.

Walt Alston was always the boss, without a question. But I've felt that he could have led us more. Alston goes on the theory that the best thing you can do when things get critical is nothing. The theory must be right for him because it's worked. The idea is that by allowing the event to take its course, you eliminate other potential sources of error. Of course, some people call that indecisiveness.

When I say that Alston could have led us more, I mean that he could have put more pressure on the club, pushed us more, driven us, simply given us more leadership. Of course, leadership also involves making the right decision at critical moments.

I think back to 1961, when we lost out to Cincinnati in the stretch. Maybe we needed some luck—everybody needs luck—but I think mainly we needed more drive from the top. Maybe we'd have lost anyway. Maybe destiny can outsmart any manager.

In '62, with seven games left on the schedule, we were four games out in front. That should have been a comfortable margin. Instead, we ended up tied with the San Francisco Giants, and we were forced into a play-off.

In the final game of the play-off we were in Dodger Stadium, and in the top of the ninth we were ahead, 4–2. I had just stolen my 104th base. This was in our half of the eighth inning. I had slid into third, the ball went wild into left field, and I went on home. When I ran into the dugout, there was excitement that I'd never seen before on a baseball field or anywhere else. It was unbelievable.

People were screaming. The players pounded each
other on the back and whooped and hollered with joy.
One more half inning and we'd be in the World Series.
There were reports that it would be the richest World
Series ever. Someone had figured it out that the play-
er's share would be a record $12,000 a man.

The Yankees had won the pennant in the American
League with people like Roger Maris, who had broken
Babe Ruth's home run record the year before, Mickey
Mantle, Yogi Berra, Tony Kubeck, Bobby Richardson,
a super team. What a Series it would be! They had the
big bats. We had the pitching with Sandy Koufax, Don
Drysdale, Roger Craig, Ron Perranoski, Johnny
Podres, and we had the speed. It would be a classic
match and the first World Series ever in new Dodger
Stadium. We could feel it in our bones, and it was
wonderful.

Then our pitching ran into trouble, and the Giants
went ahead. We had Don Drysdale out in the bullpen
ready to go. But Alston decided to save him for the
World Series. Instead, he brought in Stan Williams, a
big right-hander who was known for his wildness. The
Giants went on to win, 6–4.

Hell, we even had the chilled champagne in our
clubhouse. During the game they had carted that
champagne back and forth, from our clubhouse to the
Giants' clubhouse. By the end of the eighth inning the
caterers felt safe in assuming that it belonged to the
Dodgers. Then they had to move it back to the Giants'
clubhouse. As one of the writers said later, Madville
had turned to Mudville.

The door to our clubhouse stayed locked for half an
hour after the finish of the game. I remember sitting at
my locker, staring down at my spikes. We were all too

numb to think, too numb to feel. The game had ended late in the afternoon. By midnight there were Dodger players still in the clubhouse, sitting at their lockers, still unbelieving and tearful. I don't think I've ever seen a more desolate place in my life.

"We have no excuses," Alston told the press. He blamed nobody. He said we didn't really lose the pennant in that one afternoon, but we'd gone flat in the previous week, and that's when we booted it. In a sense, all this was true. Still, it's a matter of record that he didn't put in Drysdale in the ninth inning. Maybe the Giants would have pounded the hell out of Drysdale. But I would still have liked to have seen him out there when we needed him. I just wish Alston hadn't saved him for the junior prom that never happened.

Briefly, for the 1971 season, we had Dick Allen on the club. A tremendous ballplayer, Dick Allen marches to a different drummer, as they say, but I'd like to have eight others on my team marching to that same drummer when they go to the plate.

Dick is a complex man. He's never on time for anything, and he's not an easy ballplayer to handle. Dick's ways angered Alston. As the team captain I went to Walt to express the players' feelings that Allen, even though he may be wrong, shouldn't be disciplined.

"Skip, it could blow our chances," I said. "We need Allen at his best."

Alston looked uneasy. "We'll see what happens," he said.

Allen played, without being disciplined, and we came within an inch of winning the pennant. We lost out on the final day of the season. We won our game, against Houston, but the Giants beat the Padres in San Diego, and that put us a full game out of first. But if Alston had laid into Dick Allen, I'm sure that we would have been out of contention three weeks before the end of the season.

Over the years we had a few disputes, the skipper and I. One time Alston gave us approval to put together a committee of four—John Roseboro, Dick Trescewski, Don Drysdale, and myself—and we were given authority to fine any of our teammates who weren't hustling. The first fine had to be assessed against Willie Davis, who may have invented nonhustling. We fined him $25.

"Skip, we're fining Willie," I told Alston.

"No, I don't think so," Alston said. "I don't like the idea of players fining players."

"But you gave us the authority."

"I know, I know, but I don't like the idea now," Alston said.

"Well," I said, "then I don't want to be captain anymore."

I was sore as hell. Willie Davis had been fined, and now he was going around pouting, and Alston wouldn't even back us up. Before the game, at our clubhouse meeting, Alston was full of sarcasm.

"We've got a guy on the club here who's pouting," Walt told the club. I figured he meant Davis. But Alston looked at me. "Now he says he doesn't want to be captain. So he's pouting."

Now the eyes of twenty-four ballplayers were fixed on me.

"I'm not pouting, dammit," I said. "You okay the idea of a committee and the fines and all. Now you don't want to take his money. To hell with it. Let somebody else be captain and take the goddamn card up to the umpire. Hell with it."

We had some sharp words. Then he walked away. Nothing was settled. It was like that with Walt Alston. Nothing of any importance was ever resolved. He just let the problems drift away.

Once, in Florida, we were playing an exhibition game. Tommy Davis, in left field, had dogged a play. When we came in from the field, Alston didn't say a word to him. A few minutes later Alston said he wanted to sit up higher, in the press box.

"Get a better perspective up there," Walt told us.

"Good idea, Skip," I said. "Give me the lineup card, and I'll run the club while you're up there."

To everyone's surprise, Alston gave me the card. Off he went up to the press box. My first move as substitute manager was to take Tommy Davis the hell out of the game. When Alston heard the announcement on the public address system, he came storming down from the press box to the dugout.

"What in the hell is going on around here?" he hollered at me.

"Davis dogged it," I said. "You saw it yourself, Skip. He didn't want to play, so I took him out."

Alston's face was as red as a radish. "Give me the goddamn card," he said. He took the card from my hand in disgust. But I had only done what I thought Walt himself should have done.

I've been told that former Dodgers now with other clubs can read Alston like a book. They say you know when he'll try the squeeze. You know, to begin with, that he won't use the hit and run. You know that he'll sacrifice when the book calls for a sacrifice. He's not a manager who's given to hunches. He sticks to the book.

Walt has dignity. He has never knocked anybody off a barstool. He's good with the press. He doesn't complain in public. He doesn't cause waves. And he knows his baseball. Walt Alston might even be the great manager that some people say he is if he could communicate what he knows. Managers like Charlie Dressen and Leo Durocher were never modest about telling you what they knew. I feel certain that Alston knows a good 40 percent more baseball than he's ever been able to explain to his players.

A part of this lies in the Alston manner. A Durocher or a Dressen would holler, "Sacrifice!" Alston, in the same situation, would say, "Mmmmm, I think we should have a sacrifice now." As players we would have the feeling that Alston wasn't all that sure of his own instincts even when he was right.

Alston communicates with his players in his own subtle way. Maybe his way might be too subtle. Walt used to say to the players, "My door is always open." But very few of his ballplayers ever visited him in his office.

I knew one player who went into Walt's office with a personal problem and came out feeling worse. Alston is a kind man, and he was sympathetic, but his reserve wouldn't allow him to release his true feelings. This must have been frustrating for him, a man of inherent decency, and he was unable to help one of his players.

Contrary to popular belief, Alston has a good sense of humor. Speaking at sportswriters' dinners, he'd have his own spot, and he could hold his own with the quipsters. He'd get up before the microphone, clear his throat, and say something like "Well, it's nice to be back in Los Angeles. Been gone all winter in Darr-town, and it's nice to see all the freeways again—they're as scary as ever. Home in Darrtown we go down the streets at five miles an hour. Darrtown's a pretty small town, y'know—it's so small the main street goes through a car wash."

He would go on like that, picking up his laughs, and he'd finish with: "Well, I guess I'm expected to win the pennant this year, and I suppose I'll end up being fired in the fall again, just like always."

Audiences used to break up at Alston's dry humor. But his natural look has never been a smile. Perpetual frown marks run across his forehead. Even when the Dodgers win, very rare that you'll see any pictures in the paper of Walt Alston smiling.

I've always felt that Walt's humor has its geographic limits. Away from the ball park, on the team bus or on the plane or in a hotel lobby or waiting for transportation in a group, Walt could make amusing observations. But once he's in the ball park, he puts on his frown, his game face. And if the Dodgers had lost a game, it would never be Alston who would clear the air with a joke. On the other hand, I can't say I know of many other managers who do that either.

Alston may work in the big cities, but there's a lot of country left in him. He doesn't care much for modern gadgets. In 1970 we voted to take the money that had been collected from the players in fines and we bought two big heavy-duty hair dryers for the clubhouse. When he saw the hair dryers being installed, Alston shook his head sadly. "Hair dryers," he said. "What's the game coming to?"

At least 90 percent of the team used the dryers after a shower. Walt would look at his players under the dryers with disapproval. "Goddamn," he'd say. "I sure hope you guys look pretty enough."

"Try it, Skip, you'll like it."

"Damn pretty boys," Walt would say.

It seemed to me there was another personality imprisoned inside of Walt Alston waiting to be freed. But his Ohio inhibitions prevented him from changing. I'd bet anything Alston would like to be more Southern California in his style. His Ohio cells just wouldn't permit it.

I like to imagine Walt Alston with a mod mustache and the mod-styled hair. If Dick Williams could do it—and Dick had a crew cut just a few years ago—then so could Walt Alston. Every so often, out of the corner of my eye, I'd catch Walt as he looked at some of the young mod Dodgers, dressed for the night, and he would have a wistful, almost envious look.

Little by little, Alston did change—but not by much. From the straight conventional Ohio pants legs, he graduated into a pair of stovepipe flares.

"Like 'em?" Walt said, when he came into the clubhouse wearing his first pair of flares.

The players nodded. "Terrific, Skip." Alston liked that.

Gradually, we saw Alston go from his dark, gloomy alpaca sweaters to brighter colors in his sweaters and his sports jackets. Maybe it isn't important how a big-league manager dresses. Did anyone care how John McGraw wore his clothes? Or Joe McCarthy or Bill McKechnie? But those were different times, long before the Peacock Generation of modern man. In the last ten years or so style seems to have more meaning as a reflection of a man's personality.

Besides, clothes are important to major-league players, all of them young and with money to spend. It may be one way that a manager can feel closer to his players, by sharing one of their interests.

As time passed, Walt traded his severe Ohio clothes for the Southern California double-knits. In the process I think he was able to let something of himself out of the shell. One year he was fascinated by the motorcycles that Duke Simms and I used to ride. Alston bought two medium-size Hondas, one for himself and one for his teenage granddaughter. But he never rode his Honda in Los Angeles. He'd go trailing in the off-season in the hills of southern Ohio, around Darrtown. But I don't ever expect to see Walt Alston on a motorcycle, wearing a black leather jacket with an eagle on the back, long hair flowing in the breeze. No way.

When I was traded back to the Dodgers from Montreal in the summer of 1969, I suspect the deal wasn't made entirely with Alston's approval. It's a feeling I've never been able to shake. We shook hands. Walt congratulated me, and he said, "It's nice to have you back with us." We posed for pictures. On the surface, it was a nice welcome.

About a third of the way into the season in 1970, I almost broke my ankle sliding into second base in Cincinnati. For the rest of the year, I was a one-legged ballplayer. I still played, but my batting average took a dip. The next year the Dodgers cut my salary, the first time that had ever happened in my big-league career. But after the 1971 season, when I came out as the major-league shortstop of the year, the club restored my cut and gave me a raise.

At spring training in '72 I found myself getting splinters on the bench as Billy Russell, a rookie shortstop, played most of the time. Alston's reasoning to the press was this: Wills gets hurt, we have to know what Russell can do; we have to give him game time experience.

I kept asking Alston, "Hey, Skip, when do I play?" He told me to be patient, that I'd play when the schedule took us to Arizona and California. Then there was a players' strike, and the exhibition games were canceled. I never did play that spring. It was obvious to me that I was falling behind. Even though I started on opening day, Billy Russell was in there later, supposedly to give me some rest that I didn't need.

Soon Russell was on a streak, getting two, three hits a game. By July it was clear that I had lost my job to the rookie. Ross Newhan wrote an article about it in the Los Angeles *Times*. It was headlined IT'S HUMILIATING. It sure was. I ended up on the bench as the club's designated pinch bunter. I had told Newhan how humiliating it was to sit in Dodger Stadium, still physically able to produce, yet unable to get into the lineup. I don't think Alston liked some of my quotes, but outwardly he was cordial.

On three occasions he said to me, "Don't you worry, Maury, you'll always have a job. I'll see to that." He told me the club was having a series of meetings to plan for next year, and he said I could feel secure. From other sources I learned later that the word at the meeting was: "Wills has had it."

At the end of the season two coaching jobs came up on the Dodgers. Terrific, I thought. I was ready to coach. I had managed in winter ball in Mexico, in Hermosillo, and we'd won the pennant there. I knew that I had leadership qualities. I had been the team captain, the guy they went to when they wanted a young player to be inspired or bumped. Coaching would be ideal.

But the Dodgers brought in Tom LaSorda and Monty Basgall for the jobs, and they told me I was bypassed because they needed somebody who could "relate to the kids." Relate to the kids? What the hell did they think I'd been doing?

Yet there was never anything personal between Alston and me. Still, I know that he never forgets and he never forgives. With my arrogance and my outspokenness as a ballplayer, I know I couldn't have been easy for any manager. I don't think Walt Alston ever forgot that, and I don't think he ever forgave me for it either.

11

Umpires

IF there's a natural rivalry in the game, a baseball version of the mongoose and the cobra, it would be the uneasy relationship between manager and umpire. A player may always complain about an umpire's judgment, but when his argument grows futile or he might be ejected, it is the manager who must step in with the heavy artillery of reasoned debate. Generally, I wouldn't rate myself a fan of umpires. But I will concede that umpires are truly a part of the game, like the charley horse.

I think it was Silk Laughlin, the old umpire, who once said about his job that you can't beat the hours. They aren't bad hours, at that—about three hours or so in a day's work. In fact, the thought of being an umpire myself one day has always fascinated me. One reason is sheer curiosity. I've always wanted to see if umpiring is as difficult as some of the umpires make it seem to be. The second reason cuts deeper, and it stems from all my years of watching umpires I would judge as—there is no other word—incompetent.

I'll turn that into a flat statement: Give or take a few, one-third of all the umpires in the National League are incompetent. Not dishonest or faulty of vision or prejudiced—but incompetent, lacking in talent, ability,

225

savvy. It is a statement based not on rumor or hearsay, but strictly on my own observations from twenty-two years as a professional baseball player, including fourteen seasons in the National League, and as an NBC baseball commentator since 1973.

Therefore, I'm speaking here only of the National League, from 1959 to the present. I'll let someone else judge the umpires in the American League.

It's a problem whose roots run deep. Incompetence has become a continuing format because of all the cronyism and politics going on in the selection of major-league umpires. As one example, consider Emmett Ashford, the first black umpire in the big leagues and, in a sense, the Satchel Paige of the umpires. By that I mean that Emmett, like Satchel before him, finally did get tapped for the majors but not until age had nibbled deeply into his effectiveness. For years, Emmett Ashford worked the Pacific Coast League, where he eventually became umpire in chief. He was a dynamic calliope of a man, full of zest and high spirits, and the only umpire I know of who could draw fans into the ball park. To the fans, he was exciting, colorful, fun to watch. Baseball said he was a "showboat." Baseball has a lot to learn about the difference between showboating, which is artificial and strained, and true showmanship. Emmett Ashford was no showboat; he was a showman and a very competent umpire.

Now the result, year after year, of the selection system is painfully obvious. You have umpires who know a few basics, but they aren't really equipped with the necessary skills, and they are the ones, if you look closely, who are always out of position to judge a play. They are the ones who make erratic calls. They are the ones who let a game slip out of control. They are the ones who can't give you a legitimate reason for a call. Umpires, all too many of them, have a parent complex. "Why is he out, ump?" "Because I said so. Play ball." I call that incompetence. Umpires have always felt they were underpaid. Maybe they are underpaid, and maybe that's why they have to bring in so many incompetents. You get what you pay for.

Where incompetence shows up most often is behind the plate. This has to be the most demanding, the toughest spot of all, working home plate, with first base next in line. Umpires in the major leagues are rotated clockwise in assignment. That is to say, one game they may be assigned behind the plate, the next game they move to third, and so forth. But the big challenge lies at home plate, to stay in there behind the catcher. If you get a camera close-up, you see many an umpire flinch when the ball hits the catcher's glove. Ever so slightly, the umpire will turn his head as he flinches, and his line of vision is altered, and he blows the call.

It isn't easy to stand there with the ball smoking in at a hundred miles an hour, or close to that, and you've got a catcher in front of you and a guy with a bat swinging in front of *him*, and you just can't properly see the play. It can be extremely dangerous with someone like a Sandy Koufax or Nolan Ryan throwing the ball out of a cannon and maybe the catcher is an uncertain rookie. I'm not talking about cowardice, a fear of being hit. It is simply an inability to stand behind the plate and function at top level. There are so many unprotected vulnerable spots. You don't have a glove; you don't have a bat. You're just there—and that chest protector isn't worn to keep you from getting hurt. It's worn to keep you from getting killed.

I've seen umpires get hit in the throat by a speeding

ball tipped from a bat. I've seen them get their masks knocked right off their faces. I've seen them hit in the chest, and the blow knocks them to their knees, writhing in pain. They've got shinguards, the steel toe-plated shoes, and the jock cup. But they should be wearing armor. I've often wondered why the National League umpires don't wear the balloon type of chest protector they have over in the American League. They offer much more protection.

With my one in every three judgment of incompetence and with the law of averages, you'd be surprised how often one game can bring together a disproportionate number of lemons. And all too often it happens in a vital game. The Dodgers would be going against the Giants, we'd be at each other's throats for first place in the heat of late August, and we'd stand on the dugout steps and look out with disbelief at the umpires the league had assigned. We'd ask each other why the league couldn't switch crews, bring in the top umpires for the top game. Would it hurt the feelings of some of the incompetent umpires to be shifted to a lesser game? It probably would. But who pays the price for this kind of traditional lack of flexibility? The teams, the fans, the game, baseball itself. It's too steep a price for a few hurt feelings.

They talk about the integrity of umpires, and I won't argue with that, even though integrity has nothing to do with competence. Only once have I ever questioned an umpire's integrity, and this goes back to 1971 and the umpire was Stan Landes.

Let me tell you about Stan Landes. He's always been known as a guy who was carrying a chip on his shoulder, and on this day that chip must have weighed a ton. As the last notes of the national anthem were wafting out of Dodger Stadium, he started glancing over at the dugout; that's a sure indication of an umpire who's scouting for trouble. He's telling you by that look that he'd like to throw somebody out of the game.

We're playing the Giants, and we're all tensed up. It's a typical Dodger-Giants war, a steamy summer's night, a huge crowd and a lot of yelling. Now the one thing an umpire dislikes is for a batter to turn around in the box to question a call. And if you're a popular player in your home park and you turn around to the umpire, he knows that little move might also turn the fans on him. It's the simple act of turning around that sets off the fuse. Stay in position, face straight ahead, and you're entitled to a few words. But don't turn around. This goes for catchers, too. It's one of the unwritten rules. It's part of the baseball book.

So I'm at the plate, and the first pitch comes in low. Big-league umpires will generally call out the strikes, whereas a silent gesture means a ball. "Strike," says Landes, clicking his indicator.

"Lousy call," I snapped, looking straight ahead.

Landes pulls his mask from his face. "None o' your lip, Wills," he says.

With those words, he was taking away my basic right as a ballplayer to dispute a call. Now my teeth are clenched. I grip the bat tighter. The crowd is hollering.

The next two pitches were even lower than the first one. They were so obviously out of the strike zone— low and away—but Landes gives the strike call on both of them. And he did it, I know, just to take it out on me for questioning his first call. It is the only time in my entire career I have known an umpire to do that to me.

I didn't say a word, and I didn't look back at him. With just one quick turn-around look, I'd have been out of there, and I knew the club needed me in the ball game. There's nothing worse than being thrown out in the first inning in a game with the Giants.

I slammed my bat in the rack. The dugout crackled with anger. Everybody on our club knew what had happened, that he had purposely called me out. I was hitting right-handed, and the catcher had to lean way over to the side, away from me. So it was obvious to every ballplayer on both teams, the managers, the coaches, and I imagine a lot of the fans—and all the umpires, too, his own peers. Everybody knew. And I'm sure he knew that they knew.

There's a sequel to this story. One night, about a week later, I was having dinner with Walter Matthau, the actor, who's a big sports fan. I was still angry about what had happened against the Giants, and I passed the details along to Walter.

When I finished, he threw back his head and laughed.

"What's so funny?" I said.

"Landes," said Matthau. "That's what's funny. I knew him as a kid back in New York. He was a fat little chubby kid, Stan Landes. We used to play ball in the old neighborhood on Fifth Street. We all called him Fatso, and we ran him off the team and made him sit on the sidelines because he was too fat to play. I bet that's how he became an umpire, because we wouldn't let him play ball with us. Old Fatso Landes!"

I said, "Thanks, Walter."

Now we're in San Francisco later in the year, in Candlestick Park, and it's Dodgers and Giants again and the usual smoldering excitement, and Stan Landes is umpiring at first. It's late in the game, and there's a squeaker of a play at first on one of the Giants. It may have been Bobby Bonds. I had made a good throw on a hard grounder, but Landes gave it the safe signal. I trotted over to talk to our first baseman, Wes Parker.

"Wes," I said, "he was out, wasn't he?"

"Sure," said Wes. "Close but out."

"Why didn't you tell the umpire?"

Wes just shrugged. He never was much for complaining over decisions.

I turn toward Landes and he lifts his hand like a traffic cop. His eyes are very narrow now, like two tiny slits of ice.

"One more step, Wills, and you're out of here," he said.

Well, I took that step, and one word led to another, and out I go. And that's when I laid Matthau's story on him. "You were a fat little kid in New York," I said, taunting him, the words popping out like firecrackers. "You couldn't make the team then, and you're fat now!"

He turned purple—fat and purple.

After that, whenever the players wanted to harass Stan Landes, they'd yell, "When does the balloon go up?" They'd holler, "Hey, look at the whale!"

Then he'd turn purple again, and if he couldn't find out who said the words, he'd throw out the guy on the team that he didn't like, and that could have been any one of twenty-five players. Walter Matthau, I thank you.

Now I'll offer an example on the other side. Tom Gorman, a first-rate umpire and one of the best speakers I know of on the after-dinner circuit, asked me one day for an autographed baseball glove. He wanted a present for his grandson. I got him a brand new $30 Spaulding glove. I autographed it and gave it to Gorman. That night—I believe it was in the first inning—I went into second base on a steal. I thought I had slid under the throw, but I looked up and there was Tom Gorman with his thumb pointed upward.

"Out?" I said, astonished at the call. "How can you call me out? I was safe, Tom."

"No, no, Maurice, you were out."

We stand there, going at it toe to toe, and finally—I knew I shouldn't say it, but I said it, anyhow—I said, "Tom, I just gave you a brand-new thirty-dollar Spaulding glove for your grandson."

Gorman nodded. "I'm sorry, Maurice, you were out," he said.

He wasn't about to let the fact that I had given him a new glove influence his decision, and I appreciate that. And the truth is, if an umpire as good as Tom Gorman calls me out, I guess I might have been out.

I've always maintained that you can condition an umpire to react in your favor. But you can't do it with the present of a glove. One way to condition an umpire is by hustling. Let's say you hit a soft grounder to the infield and you leg it down to first base, giving those ninety feet everything you've got. You hustle, and you're still thrown out by five feet. Next time you hit another grounder, and you're thrown out by three feet. Now the next time at bat there's a really close play—bang, bang—and the umpire says you're safe. Why? Because he saw you bust your butt those first two times, and he's already thinking in your favor. He's conditioned, and you get the nod.

I know this is true because it happened to me when I was stealing all those bases. You can look it up. On just about every close play I was called safe. I really was safe, but many of the plays were so close there's no way an umpire could be good enough to say he saw the play with that degree of accuracy. I've had infielders make a tag at me and miss me by a fraction of an inch, and the umpire was in a position where there's no way possible for him to see it. But he'd call me safe because I'd stolen so many bases. This is a way of saying that you are preceded by your reputation.

On the other hand, later on in my career—in the twilight, as they say, it didn't have to be a fraction of an inch. The second baseman might miss me by two inches.

"You're out!" says the ump.

"Out?" I tell him. "Why am I out? You used to call me safe on the same play."

"Well, Maury," says the ump, "you aren't stealing the way you used to."

That's a true story. It happened just like that several times with different umpires saying approximately those same words.

Now we go back to 1962, which was the year that I stole 104 bases to beat Ty Cobb's record. We're in Wrigley Field in Chicago. Dick Bertell is catching for the Cubs. Bertell was one of the tougher catchers in the league for me, even though 95 percent of the time it's not the catcher but the pitcher that you steal on. But the throwing ability of the catcher may dictate to you just how good a jump you really need on the pitcher. When I first came into the league, Smokey Burgess was with the Pirates. Smokey could swing the bat, but he didn't get his nickname from his arm. He had no arm at all, which meant that I could take a shorter lead on the pitcher and still have a good chance of stealing the base.

Dick Bertell, on the other hand, could throw—

although not as good as Joe Torre of the Braves, who was the toughest catcher for me to run against. This is something I can talk about now that I'm Maury Wills, ex-Dodger and retired shortstop. While I was playing, I made it a part of my code never to knock or praise a catcher or a pitcher. Now, for instance, I can say that Warren Spahn, with his cunning left-handed moves, could give me trouble. But the minute you knock or praise a player, he's going to rise to the occasion. If you say he's good, you've upped his confidence. Tell the world he's easy to steal on, and he says to himself, "Who the hell does Wills think he is?" His pride is bruised, and you may pay the price.

Anyway, there's Bertell behind the plate. Andre Rodgers is at shortstop. I'm poised at first, ready to steal. I take a good lead, and I'm off flying. I'm about fifteen feet from the bag, set to go into my slide, and the ball is still twenty feet away. Rodgers is waiting, and I'm starting my slide, and Jocko Conlan, a fine little umpire, comes tearing in, and he's yelling, "Safe!"

I'm not even there yet, and I know the ball isn't there. So Rodgers takes the throw and follows through with the play even though he's already heard Jocko's call.

"Jocko," said Rodgers, "how in hell could you call him safe before he's even got here?"

Jocko was always a bantam rooster type of umpire. "Rodgers," he said, "you haven't got Wills out all year. What makes you think you're going to get him out now?"

Then he turned to me. "You're safe, Wills." Then to Rodgers: "Now get outa here and let's play ball."

That's what I mean by conditioning an umpire. Some players try to condition umpires with a smile and sociable words. They'll say, "How are you feeling today? How's the family? Know any good restaurants in town?" You may have a nice conversation, but you won't score any points in conditioning. The only way you condition an umpire is by your actions on the field. An umpire isn't there to judge your character—it doesn't matter if you're a gentleman or a rowdy. A player like Pete Rose, going at full throttle all the time, can have a lot going for him as far as umpire conditioning is concerned.

There's a story about umpires they tell at baseball banquets. I've heard it so often that it's beginning to sound true. It's about the umpire at third base who's watching the runner come barreling in with a triple. It's a close play, and the umpire makes the out signal, throwing his thumb in the air—but what comes out of his mouth is: "Safe!" The runner hears the safe call, and he stays on the bag.

"What are you standing there for?" says the umpire. "You're out."

"But, ump, you called me safe."

"Listen," the umpire says, "only you and me and the third baseman here heard that, but forty thousand people saw me give the out sign. So you're out." And so he was, too. Or so the story goes.

I've never heard of an umpire actually saying that, but I've seen similar instances. It's embarrassing for umpires, and it's their own fault. Umpires, most of them, make their calls too quickly. It may be tradition or some kind of false pride. Or it might be what ball-players call overhustling. A player belts a single, and in the joy of getting a hit, he gets carried away with himself, and he's going to make a double out of a single, and he's thrown out at second by ten feet. That's overhustling.

Umpires seem to be bound by some kind of unwritten rule of haste. I've never seen anything wrong with an umpire taking a good look at a play and permitting himself, say, two seconds for a call. Two seconds can be a long time. But umpires want to blurt it right now, and sometimes this causes them to make calls they really didn't mean.

I've seen it happen. A guy hits a two-hopper to the shortstop, the ball is whipped to first, and you figure, with a good throw, the runner should be out by at least a half step. He's assuming these are major-league players performing a major-league play, and in his mind there's a prejudgment forming. And then the throw hits the dirt or, possibly, the first baseman momentarily juggles the ball. But the runner gets the out call because the umpire has been conditioned. He's been caught off guard, and now he's got to adjust, and I think some of them may not be able to adjust that quickly.

Usually I will remember every detail of an encounter with an umpire, but there was a time in Milwaukee, in the old County Stadium. . . . My blood was so angered up the details are still blurred in my mind. The umpire was Lee Weyer and I had done something arrogant—I have to admit that I was rather an arrogant ballplayer. Lee called me out on a steal at second, and of course, I thought I was safe. My protests got vigorous, and out I went.

In Milwaukee the umpires had to walk right past the door of the visiting clubhouse. So I stood there by the door and waited after the game. My plan, which was my first mistake, was to tear him apart—me with my 163 pounds and my grand height of 5 feet 10, stretched. Lee Weyer stands 6 feet 6 and weighs at least 230 pounds, a giant. My second mistake is that when he walked by, I leaped out at him and started swinging. Several of the Dodger players grabbed me and pulled me away. Lee gave me the annoyed look of a rhino that had been attacked by a flea, smoothed out his ruffled lapels, and walked on. It was not my proudest moment in baseball, but it was my first and last such outburst.

If I were to judge the umpires, I would give top marks to Shag Crawford, Tom Gorman, Ed Sudal, who has individual moves I wish the other umpires would imitate, Chris Pelekoudas, and Doug Harvey as the best in my time. In fact, if I ever turn to umpiring, which is unlikely, I would pattern myself after Doug Harvey. I can remember starting arguments with Doug, and he would say, "Oh, come on, Maury, you know we're better friends than this." And he'd walk away, leaving me speechless—but still in the game.

Doug has a way about him that puts the cover on the boiler. He knows how to prevent disputes. He will always take the time to explain his decisions. He gives sensible answers. He has patience. And most of all, he has the respect of all the players in the league.

I would want a part of Shag Crawford, too, in my umpire's makeup. Shag is the Kissinger of the umpires, a tremendously skilled diplomat on the field. It was Shag who was behind the plate during the famous bat-swinging incident involving John Roseboro and Juan Marichal, and only Shag could have kept the tempers from exploding into World War III.

I remember one game—this was '71, and we're playing the Phillies in old Connie Mack Stadium. I'm at first with a single. Our pitcher—it may have been Claude Osteen—was on second. The next batter hits one sharply out to short left field. I'm figuring what the

Phils might be figuring, that with a slow runner at second—pitchers are usually slow runners—they'll go for the play at home. So I burrow in and head around second full speed for third. As I'm running, I glance quickly at the throw coming in from short left, and I don't like what I see. The ball is winging in so low it's got to hit me in the head.

At that moment I ducked so the speeding ball would miss me. Instead, the ball dipped as I ducked, and it smacked me on the leg. Shag Crawford calls me out for intentional interference.

"What?" I holler. "Intentional interference? You mean to tell me I could let that ball hit me without breaking my stride?" My point was that I wasn't trying to get hit and prevent the throw from nipping off the run at home.

Shag was as calm as a cathedral. "Now, Maury," he said, quietly, "you do have the ability to do these things."

I just stared at him. I was in no mood for compliments. Shag stayed calm, but I started yelling and jumping around, and soon I was out of the ball game. Three Dodgers had to hold me back. I was a hopping little bundle of fury.

Later, in the clubhouse, after I had simmered down, I said to myself, "Hey, that's real nice of Shag, to think I'm that smart a ballplayer." Then I started to feel badly about my behavior. I found a pencil and paper, and I wrote a note and sent it over to the umpires' room. What I wrote was: "Shag, I feel terrible that this thing happened. I was wrong in the way I comported myself. I'd like to apologize." I signed it "Respectfully, .Maury." And Shag sent back a note saying that it was an unfortunate situation and that we're still friends.

This may be the first time, to my knowledge, that a ballplayer and an umpire ever exchanged notes. Maybe, now that I think of it, it's a better way than exchanging words. By the time you write a note tempers have cooled, and you're less likely to put down the words that can get you kicked out of ball games. Give pencils and paper to the players and the umpires? Sure, why not?

Or maybe each club could have a designated pinch writer. Where are you, Jim Bouton, now that we need you?

12

Tenth Inning—A Postscript: The Banjo and the Ball Parks

TO steal a pennant, you don't have to have a banjo on your knee—but it wouldn't hurt. The banjo happens to occupy a very special niche in my life. Once, when a writer asked just what the banjo meant to me, I had to hesitate because it's never easy to put complicated feelings into words.

He didn't wait for my answer. "Here's my theory," he said to me. "I think the fact that you learned to play the banjo has something to do with all the years you had to spend in the minor leagues. It has something to do with the dogged way you played baseball and the way you stole bases, as though your life depended on it. Maybe, in a strange way, it did. It has something to do with your zeal in wanting to be a major-league manager."

Then he said, "I think the banjo is the key to Maury Wills, as a ballplayer, a manager, a man."

Perhaps it is. I don't believe the banjo shaped my life, in the way that the trumpet shaped Louis Armstrong or Miles Davis, but the shape of my life led to the banjo, which is one of the most demanding of instruments.

As a card-carrying, dues-paying member of the musicians' union in Spokane, Washington, where I lived before moving to Los Angeles, I am listed in the Local 105 roster as "Maury Wills, Banjoist." When I look at the page with my name and instrument on it, I feel a touch of pride. For it says in print that I am a musician, a performer, a professional.

Most people know very little about the banjo. Historians will tell you that there was a primitive stringed instrument played in the Congo known as the *bandzu*. The banjo itself originated among the black people of the South. The banjo, an instrument that was played by slaves, is considered the only authentic American instrument, the only one not imported from Europe. And the happy, crackling sound of the banjo has always struck people everywhere as truly American.

My own interest in music was first sparked in 1958, when I was with Spokane in the Coast League. We had a utility infielder named Dick Young, who played a four-string ukulele. He would play cowboy songs about the lone prairie and riding Old Paint on the range. He'd play on the team bus, in the clubhouse, even in the dugout. We thought he was great.

It was about then that a local TV station had a promotion stunt—any Spokane player who got four hits in one game would be given one of the new transistor radios just coming in from Japan. I got my four hits and won the radio. Then I did it again and won another radio.

Dick offered to trade his ukulele for one of my radios. I said, "Fine, if you toss in a couple of lessons." Damned if it wasn't the best trade since the Yankees got Babe Ruth from the Red Sox.

Suddenly, nothing seemed so important as that ukulele. I attacked the instrument as though it were an opposing ball club to be brought to its knees. I practiced for hours on end. In time, I played well enough to entertain the team on the bus.

Six months later I graduated to a six-string guitar. Again I practiced long, tedious hours, teaching myself from an instruction book.

In the winter before spring training camp of 1960 I bought my first banjo. It was truly love at first sound, the banjo and me. But it was brutal learning to play the thing. After three grueling months, I had learned one song—"Bye Bye Blues." I played it everywhere, over and over. As the old joke goes, I was going to play it until I got it right.

The year before, in '59, I had gone up to the Dodgers in midseason and batted a respectable .260. We won the pennant, and I played every game of the World Series. When I reported to camp at Vero Beach, Florida, I was shocked to learn that I was still assigned to the minor-league barracks.

The big leaguers, the Dodgers, stayed in a separate annex. They slept two players to a room; they had private bathrooms, throw rugs on the floor, curtains on the window. In the minor-league barracks, we slept four to a room on army cots.

In despair, I went to the late Fresco Thompson, the Dodgers' farm director, and I pleaded with him. He gave me a few words of encouragement, but not much else.

I left Fresco, and I walked out past the barracks to a cluster of palm trees. I remember hearing the crickets in the warm Florida night, and I could smell the orange blossoms, and I could look up and see all the stars in the universe. I sat under a palm tree, and for more than an hour I cried like a baby.

All my frustration and anger and bitterness flowed

out with those tears, all the ache of going through eight and a half years of the minor leagues. I became a driven ballplayer, and some of that drive, I know now, came out in my feelings toward the banjo.

I literally poured myself into the banjo—and I beat out five players to become the regular shortstop. That year I hit .295 and stole 50 bases.

And in time I did learn another tune, "Goodbye Blues," but mostly I stuck to "Bye Bye Blues." One day Sandy Koufax, normally the gentlest of men, snarled at me, "You play 'Bye Bye Blues' one more time around here, and I will personally cut the strings off your banjo."

It was no idle threat. I made sure Sandy wasn't around when I practiced, and eventually I was able to expand my repertoire.

When I was rooming with John Roseboro, we had a concert going one night. I was on banjo; Tommy Davis and Roseboro played their claviettas. The clavietta is a small wind instrument with a keyboard—a combination of harmonica and accordion—and it makes a pleasant musical sound. We were playing away, and in walked Walt Alston.

"Hi, Skip," I said, without missing a note. Alston greeted us, and then he pulled one of the biggest surprises of my baseball life.

"I can play that, you know," Alston said to Roseboro.

"You can?" said John, astonished.

Roseboro gave Alston his clavietta and sat back to listen. It turned out that Walt Alston could play the hell out of a clavietta, and he did, too.

Walt had a good feeling about music. Once, when we had lost seven straight, I thought it best to give the banjo a rest. We were leaving St. Louis on the team plane during the slump, and Alston went down the aisle and called out to me, "Maury, play a few tunes. Maybe it'll perk us up."

I pulled out my trusty banjo and played "Bye Bye Blues." Alston nodded and smiled and walked back to his seat. Next time out, we ended our losing streak.

Not all the Dodgers were banjo fans. Even my room-ie, Roseboro, finally had his fill. One afternoon, during the pennant stretch of '63, we were in the Netherland Hilton Hotel in Cincinnati, and John took a walk. Without a word, he packed his bags and headed for the door.

"What's the matter, John?" I said, plunking away.

"It's either me or the banjo, dude," John said.

There wasn't much choice. John shrugged and went downstairs and checked into his own room. Now I was rooming with a banjo.

Eventually, I was able to play quite well. I'd play at the St. Patrick's Day parties that Walter O'Malley, the Dodgers' owner, threw for his friends each year. The first of his parties that I played for, I remember opening with "Bye Bye Blues," which drew a few impolite groans.

That winter I had learned to play "Peggy O'Neill" and "My Wild Irish Rose," especially for Mr. O'Malley. He must have been pleased because he patted me on the back and slipped $100 in my pocket. That's $50 for two tunes. For that one night I must have been the highest-paid banjo plunker in the world.

When Milton Berle put together an act with six Dodgers to work the Desert Inn in Las Vegas, I played my banjo, and we were, as they say in *Variety*, socko. A year later I was booked into the Sahara in Vegas. I was a headliner, sharing the bill with Jane Powell, the singer. But I wasn't so socko this time. I was still inexperienced working alone before a paying audience. The reviews said I had a cute little act, but I could sure steal bases. In other words, I was strictly a novelty act, a ballplayer who could strum some tunes.

I realized my next move would have to be down to the minors as a banjoist. My music, in that sense, was a parallel to my baseball career. I worked the smaller clubs and practiced endlessly until I could come back in style, as an entertainer instead of a novelty. In time, I was able to play such places as Harvey's Wagon Wheels at Lake Tahoe, Nevada, and Basin Street East in New York.

In Japan they do things in a small way. Even the top acts over there are booked for only three nights. I'm pleased to say that I was held over for an extra night. I never worked Sheboygan, but they loved me in Tokyo.

We became inseparable, the banjo and me. While I was with the Pirates, I had my own banjo club in Pittsburgh, called Maury Wills' Stolen Base. Dixieland is my favorite kind of music, and I would play in the Dixieland jazz spots across the country—the Brathaus in St. Louis, Your Father's Mustache in New York, the Red Garter in San Francisco.

I finally made it back to Las Vegas. I could have been booked in one of the Strip hotels, where the big stars work. Instead, I went to the El Cortez Hotel, in downtown Vegas, for a long and still continuing run. The El Cortez became my room, and it still is. The owners also operate the Vegas Club down the street. They have a Maury Wills Room there, where they put up my trophies, including the pair of spikes I wore the year I got into the record books with 104 stolen bases.

Those are the shoes that are supposed to be on display in my name at the Hall of Fame at Cooperstown. The truth is, I didn't want to part with them. The shoes advertised as mine at Cooperstown aren't mine at all— they are the shoes that Jim Gilliam of the Dodgers used to wear.

When the people at the Hall of Fame asked for my shoes, I explained my problem to Gilliam. I told him I wanted to borrow his shoes for a good purpose.

"You mean," said Gilliam, "that my shoes will be in the Hall of Fame?"

"Right there with Babe Ruth's bat, Jim," I said.

Gilliam smiled. "Why not?" he said. "This way they'll be there waiting for me. Am I right, Mouse?"

"You are right, Jim," I said.

I hope to be in the Hall of Fame myself someday, and when I go, my banjo goes with me.

I like to play the banjo, and I also like to look at baseball fields. Driving along the freeways of Southern California or coming from the airports into the various cities on the circuit, I find myself looking at ballfields, from Little League on up to major league. They appeal to me as a place where I have earned my living since I was in my teens, but also I find pleasure in looking at the greenery. I like the clean, traditional lines of a baseball diamond. I'll be staring at a ballfield from my car window, and then I'll turn my head to capture every last possible view before the green fades from sight.

Some baseball fields, however, I like more than others. A ball park can affect one's mental and emotional approach to a game, and there is no way that it can be explained by logic. There's no logic at all, for instance, in my distaste for the ball park in Milwaukee. The sun must have shone when I was in Milwaukee, but I have memories only of cloudy skies.

In Milwaukee they'll talk about the difference between Schlitz and Michelob or how the Packers tore up the Bears, but there is rarely much talk about baseball. Even in the lobby of the Schroeder Hotel, where the visiting clubs stay, they wouldn't recognize a ballplayer if he had his name printed on his back.

The personality of the ball park reflects the personality of the town, which is bland and unexciting. Don't even ask about the girls in Milwaukee. They all look as though they had just landed fresh off the farm, and their style in clothes must have come out of *Field and Stream*.

Chicago is a different story. Chicago, that toddlin' town, swings with major-league restaurants and places to go and music to hear. Baseball is also played in Chicago as it should be played—during the day. Phil Wrigley, owner of the Cubs, dislikes night baseball, and he has never installed lights.

Mr. Wrigley is right. No matter how powerful the field lights may be, you can't beat God's own sunlight. The heat of the day brings out the best in ballplayers. The tone, the mood and feeling, the entire atmosphere are more truly baseball, the way it was intended.

During a day game, even on the field, you can smell the peanuts in the stands. At night there are no smells. Baseball should have some smells. Even the sound of the crowd is different at night. It's less carefree somehow.

But even with day games, Wrigley Field isn't easy for ballplayers. Late in the day a tricky, gusty wind comes tearing in from Lake Michigan. At four in the afternoon in Wrigley Field, look around and you don't have to be told why Chicago is known as the Windy City.

The groundkeepers never helped much either. Players always complain that the grass is maintained too high and the level of the infield isn't true, causing the ball to take some strange and unexpected hops.

Ball parks really do have their own personalities. I think of Candlestick Park in San Francisco as the last angry man. Candlestick has no affection for ballplayers. Unlike the city itself, the park is cold, indifferent, forbidding. Candlestick practically dares you to play baseball. In Candlestick it's almost always cold and unpleasant, and there are the fog banks from the bay and the wind that blows in impossible swirls. Outfielders in Candlestick should get combat pay.

At Candlestick there's an unwritten rule—no tobacco chewing by the infielders. All it takes is a stiff wind to blow him around, and he's got to squirt the outfielders with tobacco juice.

Lately, a number of more modern ball parks have been built, and some of them have all the charm of a hospital stairway. They lack warmth and tradition and memories. But the new Three Rivers Stadium in Pittsburgh does have a bit of spark. And I like River Front Stadium in Cincinnati and Busch Stadium in St. Louis. Once, in St. Louis, a young white couple came up to me with a small child. They told me they had named him after me—first name Maury, middle name Wills. I thought that was pretty nice. In fact, I was flabbergasted.

Atlanta has a ball park that is undeniably attractive, but it's devoid of any character. It reminds me of a ballplayer who has outstanding talent but no personality, the kind of player who walks into a crowd and nobody asks for his autograph.

What I liked most about the old ball parks, like Connie Mack Stadium in Philadelphia, is the closeness of the stands and the sound of the fans. The stands in the old parks were built at an angle of 60 degrees, a sharp slope. In the new parks the stands rise more gradually, at about a 45-degree angle. The fans are much farther from the action.

Maybe they weren't the last word in fancy architecture, but the old ball parks were compact and unified, and I miss them. Old Forbes Field in Pittsburgh was like that, a grand old ball park, a tobacco-chewing ball park. On the other hand, I never felt comfortable in old Crosley Field in Cincinnati. There was about a five-foot slope in the outfield grass and not much enthusiasm among the conservative burghers of the town.

As for the Houston Astrodome, it's a peculiar place for baseball. Instead of a sky overhead, there's these big beams. There's no breeze, nothing natural in the air. The first time I set foot in the Astrodome was like being on a spaceship in the TV show *Star Trek*. Even the ground crew wore space outfits. It's very futuristic. At the Astrodome you don't know whether to bat or blast off.

I like to think of Shea Stadium in New York as the Leo Durocher of ball parks—brash and arrogant, but still with some feelings of inner warmth you might not expect. Shea is New York.

Once I was late for a game with the Mets, and I hailed a cab in Manhattan. I told the cabby, "Take me out to Shea Stadium. Get me there fast and I'll take care of you. I'm in a hurry."

The cabby turned around. Wearily, he said over his shoulder, "Everybody's in a hurry, Mac."

But the way he drove was unbelievable. He whipped in and out through the traffic, zipping through red lights. He had me there in time.

"Beautiful," I said.

"No sweat, Mac," he said.

Typical New York, I thought. Hard-boiled on the outside, but he'll go all out to help, given the promise of a big tip.

Shea Stadium is flamboyant; it's exciting and dramatic. You can hear the airliners roaring in low, heading over the right field stands into LaGuardia Field. Sometimes that's all you can hear. There are helicopters whirling in noisily on their way from Kennedy International to Manhattan. All this adds to the excitement.

At Shea you get the feeling that the pennant hinges on every play. The fans at Shea must be the most boisterous and supercharged of any since the old Dodger days at Ebbets Field. They root loudly for the Mets, but there's also a hard core of rooters in the stands whose old-time loyalty to the Dodgers has never wavered.

Shea is tension. You are always aware of the presence of the New York writers, who are the most competitive and hard-hitting in the business. You are always aware that whatever happens in New York—the hub of communications, the center of the wire services and the networks—the next day it's all over the country. New York makes reputations. The media in New York have the power to make you into a national hero or a national bum. You think of such things, in Shea Stadium.

My favorite ball park of them all is Dodger Stadium in Los Angeles, one of the few built especially for baseball. Dodger Stadium is a magnificent showplace. It's bright and cheerful; the landscaping and flowers are attractive; the ground is always well manicured; the dugouts are spacious.

Dodger Stadium is truly Los Angeles. Dodger Stadium reflects the good life and the freedom that the rest of the country has in mind when they think about Southern California. Dodger Stadium has a personality that's both casual and classy. Dodger Stadium has glamor and sex appeal. If Candlestick Park is the last angry man, Dodger Stadium is the beautiful woman of ball parks.

On an October day in 1972, soon after I'd been released by the Dodgers, I visited Dodger Stadium. I walked around alone in the empty ball park. Then I leaned on a railing, and I stared at the green field below. I felt a strange kind of loneliness.

As I stared down at the field where I had played for so much of my career, I was reminded of movies in which the past returns in a series of flashbacks, and at once the ball park became alive for me.

In the silence of the empty stadium, again I heard the voices of the fans, 50,000 strong, urging me on with "Go! Go! Go!" I thought of Walt and Leo and Sandy and Willie and Don and Tommy and Duke and big John and the rest, the fights, the good times, the pennants.

I thought of the O'Malleys, Walter and Peter, and playing the banjo at their St. Patrick's Day parties. I thought of Red Patterson's grin, Buzzie Bavasi cracking jokes. I thought of velvet-voiced Vin Scully and Jerry Doggett, the Dodger announcers, whose broadcasts helped create the image of "Little Maury" stealing bases. I thought of the team physician, wise Doc Kerlan, and how he cared.

I heard all the voices and saw all the faces.

Baseball has given me an exciting and fulfilling life with achievements I never dreamed of when I was a kid in Washington, D.C., stealing bases on the sandlots. They have been unforgettable years, and now, with my sights set on being a manager, I am looking forward to more.

What's past is prologue. Who can say what lies ahead? I'm kneeling in the on-deck circle, waiting. . . .